T0243820

WISE WORDS
for WOMEN

*words to soothe, comfort,
challenge, and inspire*

DONNA LANCASTER

This publication is designed to provide accurate and authoritative information
in regard to the subject matter covered. It is sold with the understanding
that the publisher is not engaged in rendering legal, accounting, or other
professional service. If legal advice or other expert assistance is required,
the services of a competent professional person should be sought. —*From
a Declaration of Principles Jointly Adopted by a Committee of the American
Bar Association and a Committee of Publishers and Associations*

Published by Sourcebooks
P.O. Box 4410, Naperville, Illinois 60567-4410
(630) 961-3900
sourcebooks.com

Originally published in 2023 in Great Britain by Ebury Press, an imprint of
Ebury Publishing. Ebury Press is part of the Penguin Random House group of
companies whose addresses can be found at global.penguinrandomhouse.com

Cataloging-in-Publication Data is on file with the Library of Congress.

Printed and bound in the United States of America.
SB 10 9 8 7 6 5 4 3 2 1

For my two precious daughters – Gemma and Lucy.

May this book support you in learning how to breathe underwater, and to always remember that down in the depths there are pearls to be found.

I Love you TMD WAMH. Aways xx

Contents

Introduction

Many of our ancestors used to gather around fires in their communities every evening to prepare food, cook, eat, relax and share the challenges and highlights from their day. Children, parents, grandparents, great-grandparents, aunts and uncles all came together to connect. What a beautiful ritual. During any given gathering around that fire, there might be stories shared, tears shed, jokes and laughter, scolding, reassurance and wisdom passed along. Often all of the above, along with food, cuddles and dancing.

The oldest members of the community were often the most respected and revered. Everyone knew that these wise Elders had already walked life's long and winding path, and in doing so had faced and overcome much adversity, and learned many hard-won lessons along the way. The Elders knew it was their role and responsibility to reach out a guiding and steadying hand, to support those following in their footsteps. The next generations. So, when these wise Elders spoke up at the gatherings by the fire, people in the community stopped to listen. And when they didn't speak, people listened even more.

Now, some of you may be lucky enough to still have these kinds of extended family connections, if not gathering around a roaring fire, at least around a dining table. However, for many of us this is not possible, as various family members often live far apart, even in different countries. For those of you, like myself, who come from a dysfunctional or estranged family, there might be zero access to any older and wiser family members.

We have lost many of these deeply important and connecting communal rituals that bind us. Like learning how to listen to the wisdom of the seasons, and the sun and the moon. How to respect and tend to the land, with its different plants and food sources, and how to prepare and cook produce. Along the way, we have also forgotten important initiations that these gatherings offered to support us in crossing the threshold from childhood into adulthood. No wonder so many young people feel so lost, disconnected and untethered ... because they are.

Many are still unconsciously yearning for the support and guidance of community, and specifically Elders, to help them navigate their own rocky path into and through adulthood. But who can they turn to now for this love and support? Who is there to guide and reassure them when they feel lost, confused or afraid? Who will give them a firm nudge or a 'ticking off' followed by a loving cuddle when they stray too far from the 'right' path?

Of course, some people do have their parents to lean on, but they too might be wrestling with their own challenges and struggles. Often the parents need their own 'Elder' to turn to and guide them. Without any family lineage foundation, nowadays the only thing many younger people have as an alternative 'Elder' is social media, and it seems people have a lot to say on there, although I'm not sure how much of that is wisdom! What I believe is really needed are wise Elders, and that doesn't always have to be someone related to you or part of your extended family.

Although both men and women have traditionally taken on an eldership role, in this book we focus specifically on the female Elders. Throughout history, women have been the gatekeepers of the beginning and ending of the human experience, with midwives welcoming us into the world and death doulas or daughters supporting us as we leave it. In between these two portals, it is women who share their wisdom, offering guidance and support in their respective roles as friends, sisters, mothers, grandmothers, healers and teachers. Alongside these roles, we also have the female archetypes of the witch, crone, wise woman, goddess, queen, shaman and Elder – to name a few. It is the divine feminine within each of these archetypes that nurtures, nourishes, comforts, guides and loves others into their own growth and healing.

Most of us women were born into and raised within a patriarchal system, and feel the weight of that burden that we have been carrying, even if we can't put it into words yet. As we begin to awaken from this outdated toxic masculine model, we start to reclaim our essential nature. This book is about that journey. A return for the divine truth of ourselves. It is my view as a training Elder that if the world is to be saved, it will be the divine feminine that will ultimately save us all.

So, what is an 'Elder'?

An Elder for me is someone who has grown both older *and* wiser. Many people sadly only grow older and lament the loss of their youth. Always looking backwards for what has or might have been, without taking the necessary gifts and learnings, wrapped up within their struggles, to move forwards and pass on. My parents sadly were very much like this. Perhaps yours are, too. An Elder, however, recognises that she has been on a heroine's journey. She has courageously faced both the darkness within and without her, and has wrestled many demons and dragons along the way. She has remembered that Love begins with a capital L.

During her many struggles, the Elder, whilst down in the dark waters of her life, has always picked up a lesson and brought it back with her. These precious pearls are the gifts she then commits to sharing with those who might be drowning in the shallows or still learning to breathe underwater. An Elder knows it is her responsibility and duty to share her wisdom with all those ready and willing to listen and learn.

A true Elder will Love you completely with her whole heart. Sometimes tenderly and sometimes with a splash of cold water thrown into your sleepy face. Needs must. She keeps her own ego in check, regularly seeking out embarrassing moments to ensure humility is never far. An Elder, perhaps most importantly, knows and lives pure Joy. She radiates it out across the world and every awakening Soul feels it when in her presence, or nearby. She acts like a compass, a guiding light, showing those who follow in her footsteps where to avoid unnecessary pain. (She basically shows them where the dog shit lies on the path of life!)

This little book of wise words is a collection of some of my own hard-won wisdom, acquired along the rich and messy path of my life so far. At this stage, as I write, I see myself as an Elder in training, because I'm still stumbling, getting back up, learning and expanding with each tumble. However, I do feel ready to pass on some of the wisdom that I have gained so far, as well as some that has been passed on to me by wise Elders in my own life.

This book offers a collection of short pieces of my writing, and is aimed at women of all ages and from all walks of life: young women still in school or heading off to university, women who are career-focused, new mothers, single parents, those who are retiring or those on a spiritual path. Essentially, women like you. My intention is to offer words that I hope will soothe, comfort, challenge and inspire you, as well as offering hope, love, kindness, wisdom and direction. Occasionally, these words might even feel like a little splash of cold water on your face (but always only in the name of love, I promise!). These words will, if you let them, work as a healing balm, applied to the places inside you that ache or hurt.

This book is called *Wise Words for Women* and that, of course, includes all those who identify as a woman, even if their birth certificate might say otherwise. However, if you're male, identify as male or are non-binary, you are also most welcome here and I do hope there is something within these pages for everyone. I'd say that the title is more like a dedication to women, primarily because women are simply fabulous, and they also tend to be the gatekeepers of healing and lead the way in all matters of the heart. This book has something to offer each and every one of you.

An 'Elder in your pocket'

Opening this book will be like turning to a wise female Elder to be guided, challenged and supported. Like the mother or grandmother you perhaps always wanted or needed to help you navigate your life's path. Women are increasingly turning towards books as a means of searching for some answers to the deeper meaning of life and how to navigate its challenges. The words in these pages cut to the heart of it all with short accessible pieces, covering universal topics of love, loss, healing and everything in between. Each piece is an invitation to wake up to life, beyond past hurts and traumas or current struggles. To encourage you to question your old beliefs and go deeper, and see things and your life from different perspectives. You will hear your own voice spoken within these words, even if you can't yet articulate them. Each page acting as a wake-up call, daring us all to live a bigger life than the one the world has offered us.

My hope is that you will want to carry this little book with you in your bag, keep it by your bedside or dip into it first thing every morning as you drink your coffee, when you need some inspiration or words of encouragement. It can serve as a source of support for you in challenging times or read daily to stay connected and inspired, perhaps as a personal ritual. You might wish to open it intuitively to a 'random' page and find the perfect words that you need for that day, or for this time in your life. I call this the Universe showing off! (Don't you love it when that happens?) You might also feel drawn to a particular chapter because of the topic covered and how this resonates with your own current focus or struggles. Trust your gut!

And let's be clear: this book is definitely not about giving advice, or telling you 'THE truth' or what you *must* do. It's more about offering another perspective from someone who might be a few steps further along life's path ... that's all. Because all the wisdom contained within these pages is the same wisdom you have within you! Yes, it's true. This little book will merely help guide you back to that quiet place inside and support you to listen to your own deeper wisdom, rather than the nagging voices in your head. In reading and re-reading the words that most resonate with you, you will slowly start to trust yourself once again. To view your many struggles as a necessary part of the human condition and, over time, to find the gifts that are always wrapped up within the painful bits.

It will also reconnect you to your joy (or even the possibility of it), because, yes, there are many struggles and stumbles along the road of life, but one thing I know for sure is that we must never ever forget to notice and smell the flowers. So when you fall down on your back, remember that you can also open your eyes, look up and see the stars. Or when you end up face down in the dirt of Humility Street (again), remember to smell the fresh grass or earth beneath you.

So, before you turn to the next page to fully begin this book, I invite you to take a moment to close your eyes, book resting in your lap, and imagine yourself sitting around a campfire. Smell the wonderful scent of the burning wood and hear the crackle of the fire as in your mind's eye you see the flickering beautiful colours of the magical flames. Visualise now a community of your people sitting here alongside you. Look closely at all their beautiful faces. Perhaps your own family or the family you have chosen – friends, partner, siblings, pets. Invite them all along. Once again, feel the heat of the fire on your face, warming your hands and whole body. Notice how good it feels to be here, outside in nature and in community. Breathe that in.

And as you take one final look around your gathering by the fire, you will see there, sitting opposite you, a wise Elder with a warm smile, a mischievous twinkle in her eyes and some important stories to share with you. Be still now and come closer to her, like a child, humble, open and curious. Lean in and get ready to listen carefully to what she has to say, for there may be pearls she shares here, especially for you. And if you pay really close attention, there may even be a deeper meaning for you, hidden in between her words.

And later there will definitely be some dancing ...

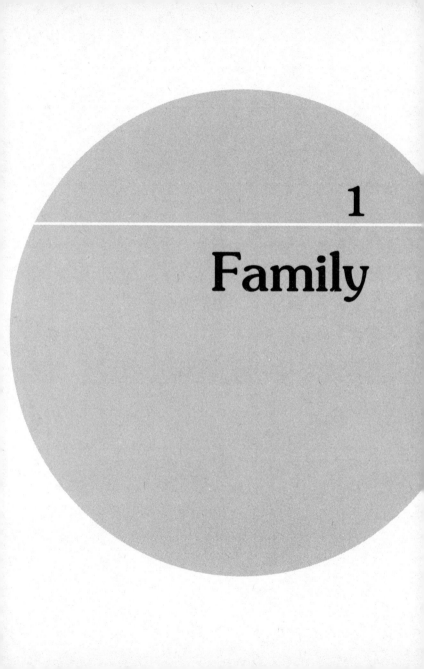

1

Family

Imperfect Love

Yesterday I took my grandson to the beach, where we collected 'emotion pebbles' and then released them into the sea, letting go of our frustrations and heartbreak with an almighty roar. We bowed afterwards to thank the sea for receiving them.

Rituals.

We played thumb wars and ate toast together, cuddling in the same chair, as we spoke of missing the people we love. We looked out of the window at the crowded beach, like two nosy parkers watching the world go by. We discussed littering and its impact on the environment. My heart ached at the beauty of it all.

Moments.

Later that same day I shouted at my grandson, when what I meant to say was: 'I'm tired, please stop doing that.'

Immediately afterwards, I invited him onto my lap, looked him in the eyes and apologised, explaining my mistake (not excusing it). I kissed his tears away and felt his little heart settle in his chest, as he heard and felt my apology, and the love wrapped up within it.

I felt guilty and forgave myself, then made a vow to do better next time. Then we played a tickle game and both farted. Imperfect Love.

Family healing

It can be really hard to be the mother you want to be, when you did not receive healthy mothering yourself. We all start out with so many hopes and dreams of how we will parent this precious little life – so different from how we were parented, for sure! But if we don't do our healing work, sooner or later we will hear our mother's words falling from our mouth towards our child. Our mother's dysfunction living on inside of us. Accompanying our own. Not so different after all.

But hear this: no mother carries a child inside her and then gives birth and looks at her beautiful baby and thinks, 'I'm going to really f*ck you up.' And yet as Philip Larkin acknowledges, we often do. We make mistakes, we shout when we should listen, we are busy cooking when they want cuddles.

Exhausted and overwhelmed, we focus on what needs doing rather than simply being. Yet we will still read that extra bedtime story when they ask, even though our Soul is screaming for space and time for ourselves. 'Where did I go?' we wonder, as we fall into a brief and restless sleep.

And then there's the shame. A shame that only a mother knows. The weight of which can destroy her life-force. All GOOD mothers share the same fears: 'What have I done? Have I really screwed them up? I'm a terrible person.'

And now, all these years later, my own daughters both thrive and struggle as parents, too. But with less of a burden to carry because we have healed together and on our own. We are closer than we have ever been because of it.

So that I can sit with my grandsons and be the Elder they need. Holding them to my chest, soft and warm. Loving them to health. And yes, they will no doubt face many struggles, as we all do. But I am comforted to know that their load will be a little lighter in this lifetime, because we made it so.

That's the power of healing work. That's what's possible. So if you haven't, I urge you. Begin.

Forgiveness –
a personal journey

1. It's unforgivable – there are no excuses for what you did.

2. I can't forgive – it's impossible, the hurt runs too deep.

3. I won't forgive – I refuse to let you off the hook.

4. I need to forgive – I recognise that forgiveness would be good for me and that it's not about you.

5. I want to forgive – I no longer wish to carry all this hurt and blame, it's exhausting.

6. I forgive you – I free myself and understand that forgiving is not forgetting.

7. There's nothing to forgive – I can honour your pain alongside my own, whilst seeing the deeper meaning of your role in my life.

8. Gratitude – I can move beyond the past to recognise the gifts I have received from the whole experience.

The apple never falls

It's a really good idea to make your peace with your parents, especially the one that hurt you the most, because sooner or later, in a myriad of ways, you will become them. (The Universe loves a laugh.)

Tribe

Eventually, there will come a day when, as we take a good long look in the mirror, we see our parents staring back at us. Not just in our face but in our whole demeanour, thoughts, beliefs and choices. Every part of us, shaped by our history.

And as we look closer, we notice *their* parents, standing behind ours in the reflection. And if we look even closer still, we see our parents' grandparents.

Back and back it goes, through the generations. All of the women and men in our family that came before us, reflected in the mirror in front of us. These are the people, for better and for worse, that we carry within us.

Our tribe.

It is up to us to gratefully make use of the many gifts we have received from our history and to respectfully discard any poisoned arrows shot into us unquestioningly by our kin. It is up to us to honour our family by living the life we have been blessed with. In love and truth.

As we gaze upon our ancestors, may we take a moment to acknowledge the huge sacrifices so many of them made so that we could be alive today, standing here gazing at our own reflection. Bare, unshackled feet connecting with the warm solid earth beneath us.

'Oh, let me be the one who breaks the chains of dysfunction in my family and, in doing so, sets us all free.'

Good enough is good enough

» I'm failing my children.

» I can't believe I just said that to them.

» They deserve so much more than I can give.

» I'm such a terrible mother.

» I don't know how to do this.

» Other mothers seem to be able to handle this.

» I'm so ashamed about screaming at them.

» Sometimes I wish I could just run away.

» Why can't I do better?!

It's only the good mothers who say these things to themselves btw.

Just so you know.

And one final thought ... 'Good enough parenting' (as defined by the paediatrician and psychoanalyst Donald Winnicott) is essentially when you meet the needs of your children more often than not.

Just so you know.

Loss

I lost my mum three times in total.

The first time was as a young child, when she was unavailable to me due to her love addiction with my alcoholic father. She was there but not there. Completely lost to me.

Secondly, I lost her as a young adult when I blamed and then rejected her, as she had previously rejected me. (Revenge, as it turned out, was not so sweet.)

Thirdly, I lost my mum when she died.

Every single time I longed for her. Every single time I missed her. All the time I have loved her.

A love so sweet

My mum loved us through sweets. She rarely cooked for us, as she was always busy working, but she left us her hard-earned money to go buy some treats. Whenever my dad beat her or us, we would awake to find Cadbury Cream Eggs and Fanta left outside our bedroom doors! Special delivery. An apology of sorts, which is another form of love.

She tried so hard to love us, my mum, from her exhausted broken battered heart. She wanted so desperately for us to know the sweetness of life and love. But it only came to us inside a chocolate egg for many years.

I still love sweet things. I still turn to them when I feel in need of comfort and a mother's love. The difference now is that, having long since made that connection, I don't have a bad word to say to myself about this. I simply place limits upon that child inside of me needing comfort. Yes, she can have the occasional sweet thing, but most importantly, she can have my true love.

A shape called tenderness

When my mum died, my heart changed shape and colour, as well as size. I physically felt it break wide open and it doubled (at least) in size overnight. Painful.

Yet I awoke the morning after her death and it felt like I could breathe so much more air into my lungs. Finally, after more than four years of waiting and wondering when death would take her, it was over. The utter relief, as well as the intense sadness, was overwhelming.

The shape my heart took on was that of tenderness. If you haven't lost a close loved one, you might not recognise this shape, but those who have, do.

And as for the resulting colour, my heart turned into the deepest shade of true Love. I now know that this was my mum's parting gift to me as she left this Earth and her Spirit flew Home. She gave me back my whole heart. Thanks, Mum.

Closure

The day I finally grew up was when I could see my mother and father as a woman and a man first and foremost. That they had a life, love and longings way before they became my parents.

When I could recognise that they were each once a little child (just like me) with hopes and dreams (just like me). When I was able to consider their pain and suffering without comparing it to my own. That they had made many mistakes because they were human (just like me).

And when I finally realised what they had sacrificed for me and the gifts that they had passed on to me, I found freedom. There was nothing left to forgive.

Lineage

Turn around, look back, see who's been standing behind you all along.

Your Ancestors.

All the women and men who came before you. Look at their faces, know their names, imagine their struggles ...

Then get down on your knees and thank them. Weep with gratitude for what they sacrificed for you. Bring food to your altar for them. Worship the ground they walked on. Their feet are also yours ...

Stand up, lean back into their arms. Feel yourself held and supported always. They have got your back. An invisible team cheering you on.

Now go, make them proud ...

2
Healing

Humility Street

Your wound is always a portal. But you need to be courageous enough to crawl through it to discover the golden gifts awaiting you on the other side. And that's always going to be painful (although not as much as avoiding the wound itself – ouch). The deal is that you can't walk or run through this portal, with your head held high, nose in the air, and neither can you swing or climb down gracefully to safety (dream on). You definitely can't go under, over or around it (although many people try). The truth is that your wound portal is deliberately shaped and sized, so that the only possible way you will fit through it is on your knees.

Stories

If you spend your whole life running, escaping and avoiding, without any time spent on reflection or inner exploration, how will you ever discover the deeper wisdom of your own Soul?

To never do any inner work is like going your whole life without reading a single book! No learning to be had, no wisdom to be discovered and no understanding of the different characters and the roles that they necessarily play in the story called 'my life'.

Without inner enquiry, how will you ever discover the magical meaning hidden in between the words of your own story? Or the simple, yet profound, truth that the ending is always a beginning, and that when all is said and done, it's only ever a story ... and you can learn to write a new one.

Falling

Sometimes you think you've hit rock bottom, but sadly it turns out that no ... not yet. You've just hit another rock. Maybe even thrown it at yourself.

Deep breath now, there is clearly further still for you to fall ...

Welcoming yourself home

To welcome yourself home means to consciously begin to embrace, accept and, eventually, love all parts of yourself. It involves returning for those aspects of yourself from childhood that you may have lost or disowned along the way.

You know that part of you that feels never good enough? You go back for her.

You remember the part of you that feels ugly and stupid? You go back for her.

And the unlovable one? Yes, her too.

So how do we actually do it? Of course it's not an overnight job, and ideally it helps to be supported in this process. But here are some things I've learned along the way ...

1. Become an 'emotional detective' in your life. Make a list of which experiences broke your heart and at what age. Record what feelings you had/have and the core beliefs you took on as a result of this. Acknowledge, for example, that there is still a four-, seven- and eleven-year-old hurt you trapped inside. They are parts of you and need you. They belong with you. It's very hard to feel whole without them.

2. Tell a trusted person about what happened to you. Dare to be safely vulnerable with others who will not try to fix you or invalidate your experience.

3. Allow your feelings to flow about what happened to you. Anger, sadness and fear all have a place. Grieve with your whole body. Hold your own hand as you do.

4. Take those young parts of you with you each day. If you have a photo of yourself at that age, pop it in your pocket and carry her with you. Say to yourself, 'Sometimes there is a part of me that feels not good enough and that's OK. I am learning to love and accept that part of me. She's welcome here.'

5. Be your own best friend. Word by word, choice by choice, day by day.

   If you do this process consistently, one day you will wake up and realise that your heart is no longer broken. You will feel its wholeness (scars and all), recognising that all parts of you are finally home.

6. You will begin to giggle ...

New arrivals

Happiness arrived for me when I changed my mind ...

No more drama

Like many of you, I grew up in an environment with a lot of drama and chaos. My father a violent alcoholic, and my mother a love addict. Rarely would a day go by when there wasn't some kind of argument or explosions of rage. In our house things got thrown and smashed up, and sometimes so did people.

It was a scary, unsafe place to grow up in, that's for sure. That's why I often call my childhood a war zone, because it certainly felt like that to a small, frightened child. Big people who were meant to love and protect us, but were instead completely out of control, and hurting each other and us.

And so, with this as a launching pad for my life, it's hardly surprising that I would go on to seek out dysfunctional relationships of my own. I had become so used to (addicted to) the high levels of activation this created in my nervous system, that it was like a drug to me.

Wherever I went, I would unconsciously seek out drama, violence and chaos. And if it wasn't there, I'd create it myself. It all felt so familiar. Painful but familiar (and that word comes from family btw). I associated love with pain and connection with hurt. It was all I knew.

And if anyone remotely healthy came towards me, I would send them packing whilst shouting, 'BORING!' at their backs. Drama indeed.

And then one day, I simply couldn't bear it (or myself) anymore, and so the healing began. I stopped making excuses and started therapy. I stayed single for more than ten minutes and joined a

12-step programme for love addiction. I finally stopped giving myself away. I stopped betraying that hurt little girl inside who needed safety and love. I came back for her.

I got well and I got healthy. I even discovered joy. Who knew?!

(And so can you.)

Embracing your inner a***hole

As many of us know, part of our healing process is to return for, and integrate, all parts of ourselves, especially those that we have rejected and judged harshly. So those parts of us that feel 'less than' or 'unworthy', 'too much' and 'shameful' must be faced, grieved and welcomed back inside of us.

Home.

Well, the same also applies to our inner a***hole. This is the part of us that carries our negative shadow. The part of us that is quite frankly a bit of a tw*t. This version of ourselves that sometimes says mean things and can be selfish, stubborn, childish, angry and unkind.

Of course it's not about letting this shadowy self run amok without consequence. We need to be mindful of keeping tabs on these aspects and rein them in as required. But what we don't do is deny, condemn or reject them. They are part of the truth of us. Our authentic flawed selves.

Embracing your IA is about peeling off those 'need to be perfect/nice/likeable all the time' masks to reveal that we, too, can be an imperfect a***hole at times. And that's OK. There's nothing wrong with that or with us. Because it's also known as being fully human. Fully imperfectly alive.

Whole.

The day I accepted that parts of me could also be rather unpleasant, I found, ironically, that my heart grew.

So here's to the inner a***hole. Both yours and mine.

Grief is love bleeding

When we cut our skin, we bleed. We know this. The blood shows us that we are hurting and that the bleeding area needs our attention. Blood plays a key role in cleaning the wound, preventing infection.

Grief is like that. It shows us that we are hurting and that the wound needs our attention. That our heart has been broken open and all the love it contains, for who or what we have lost, has begun to bleed out of us, cleansing the wound. And as we tend to it with our full attention, allowing all of our emotions and our tears, it will very slowly begin to heal. And over time the wound will close and eventually become a scar. A precious, beautiful scar.

And all that love that we bleed isn't lost. It is in fact the healing balm for the wound. Almost like the last precious gift from our lost loved ones. To expand our capacity for love.

Deeper still ...

And if you look really closely, you will see that your tears are in fact simply liquid drops of love. How beautiful.

Grief is love bleeding.

It shows that who or what we have lost matters. And sometimes that's even a part of ourselves.

It is not the price we pay for love.

Grief IS love.

So let your beautiful broken heart bleed.

Resolution

Recently, I had a falling-out with someone I love dearly. There was a misunderstanding and in the heat of the moment we both said things we didn't mean. We parted unresolved, tight-lipped and upset. Tears were shed.

That night I sat down and reflected upon the conversation, including what got triggered in me and why. I made notes. I adore this person so it felt like the least I could do. Plus, I wanted to learn from it, in order to try not to make the same mistakes again. I don't like hurting people.

The next morning, I flushed my ego down the loo and reached out to them. Without sharing the private details, this is an abbreviated version of my side of the follow-up conversation, in case it's helpful for some of you. 'I'm sorry about yesterday and some of the clumsy things I said. I didn't express myself very well and I know I hurt your feelings. That wasn't my intention. At some point my ego kicked in and I stopped hearing you. It just became about me proving I was right. And you know that thing I said? Well, I was talking about myself really and projecting that on to you. You didn't deserve that and I take it back. I think you're amazing. I love you. Please can we start again?'

And just like that, we reconnected. Resolution. No sweeping under the carpet of any unfinished business. No residual resentment or bitterness left behind. A clean slate. We started again.

Clues

Some clues that you are on a healing path:

» You no longer believe everything you think.

» You are becoming more reflective, questioning habitual ways of thinking, feeling and behaving.

» You still get triggered at times but can turn it around more quickly, returning from emotional child to adult.

» Criticism still hurts but you recover more easily and have some perspective.

» You can receive feedback without feeling criticised or the need to attack.

» You judge less – others and yourself.

» You are developing compassion for the parts of you that stumble.

» You might not love yourself (yet) but you are learning to accept and even like yourself. The rest will follow in time.

» You find you want to tell the truth more and can't be dealing with BS.

» You feel softer, more open and vulnerable.

» You cry and laugh more.

» You're curious about forgiveness for yourself and others.

» Some old relationships need refreshing or binning.

» You are becoming more boundaried.

» You've stopped taking yourself so seriously.

» Polite conversation brings you out in a rash.

When trauma speaks

When trauma speaks, sometimes she says, 'I love you,' and doesn't mean it – her need to belong is so strong.

When trauma speaks, sometimes she says, 'Please hurt me,' when really she means, 'Please hold me.' She gets confused. Sometimes.

When trauma speaks, sometimes she will lay with anyone who will have her. Anything to find a safe place to rest and a warm body to nest with. If only for the night.

Sometimes trauma will stay much longer than is good for her. At other times she will run far, far away ...

Trauma speaks the language of addiction. She'll use anything to take the pain away. (Who wouldn't?)

When trauma speaks, sometimes she will destroy everyone and everything she touches. Like the shadow of Midas. Burning her whole life to the ground. Yours, too, if you're not careful. Dark, hot coal and ash instead of shiny, solid gold.

When trauma speaks, her voice can be cold as ice. She will try to warn you to stay away, and heaven help you if you don't. Burning coals at the ready ...

Trauma might not start the war, but she will always finish it.

When trauma speaks, she can be loud and brash, withdrawn and harsh, but it's all just armour and defence. Underneath she's terrified.

When trauma speaks, her language is one of shame, guilt and blame. Unconsciously avoiding the grief underneath.

Trauma cries alone and mostly at night. Sometimes only on the inside. She's found it's safest that way.

Trauma can heal. Trauma is frozen love, and so anything warm will start the defrost. Warm people, water, hearts, touch, kindness, sunshine.

Defrosting trauma, she dares to hope that there is another way. A warmer future very different from her frozen cold past.

And she's right.

Trauma trail

People often think of trauma as something related to war veterans or victims of serious crimes, and of course this is true. But trauma also happens to children who were bullied, neglected, ridiculed or ignored. Those who were violated and felt powerless and afraid, growing up in a place that was chaotic and unsafe.

Traumatised adults grow from these children; the ones who were not listened to, nurtured, seen nor celebrated for who they were. The invisible, secret holders, black sheep and truth tellers of the family. Sadly, this relates to so many of us.

Here are a few ways in which my trauma manifested in my 20s and 30s:

» I was super independent and hated asking for help. I developed a warrior-woman persona to survive.

» I had a strong startle response, jumping out of my skin at the slightest unexpected noise.

» I was consumed with self-loathing, and put myself in a lot of risky and dangerous situations.

» I worked and worked and worked to avoid feeling the pain. It didn't work!

» I slept with anyone who would give me attention and married the first man who said he loved me. I gave myself away.

» I was loud and brash as a cover for my fears and tears.

» I rejected anyone kind and loving towards me, considering them boring and dull. Also defective, if they could dare to love me. Freaks!

» I slept with a hall/bedroom light on and was afraid of the dark for decades. Bad things happened in my childhood home at night.

» Men terrified me so I used my sexuality to gain control over them. I encouraged some of them to hit me, believing I deserved it.

» I binge drank and took drugs to cope. It was in many ways like a long, slow suicide attempt.

» I sleepwalked through my children's early years. I remember very little about raising them. This was the highest price of all.

Healing through therapy and bodywork wasn't easy nor quick. There was a lot of grief to face and it was very painful at times. But definitely not as painful as living half a life.

Slowly but surely, I recovered from my trauma. Day by day I got better and life got lighter. Healing really is possible. I promise.

Miracles

When we break a bone in our leg, we know that we need professional help and treatment for it to heal. We accept that we cannot continue as before, running around on a broken leg. 'Oh, it's OK, it doesn't hurt THAT much.' Perhaps reluctantly or even gratefully, we ask for help – allowing others to look after us, surrendering to the rest – and trust that our miraculous body will allow the bone to eventually heal.

All in good time.

If only we applied this same approach to our 'inner breaks', like when our heart gets shattered through the end of a marriage or the death of a loved one, or when we finally accept the devastating reality that we may not be able to have kids. If only we allowed ourselves to recognise that we need help and treatment for these kinds of breaks, too. Heart breaks. That we don't have to do it alone, limping around, bleeding on the inside or all over others.

If only we could accept that we cannot continue life as before. That things are different now. And that we need to stop running, to press pause and to apply love to the places that really hurt. Ouch. Recognising that the heart needs time, and the bandages of tenderness and tears, in order to heal.

And just like with a broken leg, your heart will eventually return to wholeness. Nothing short of a miracle. Perhaps even leaving behind a beautiful scar or two in its wake, just like for some there will always be a slight limp as they walk. Like a living memento of the precious gift of loss – reminding us that who or what was lost mattered. Leaving us softer, slower, more open, tender, compassionate and grateful.

All in good time.

Acceptance

When you learn to stop resisting and fighting against Life, and instead accept it (which doesn't always mean like it btw) – your body, your losses, your past, your health, your life situation and indeed Life itself – exactly as it is, ironically, everything changes. Especially you.

Worthy – a definition

'To believe that you have inherent value. A person who is deemed important and deserving of respect.'

Remembering that we are Worthy does not exclude us from feelings of sadness, anger or fear. It doesn't mean that we are floating through life with a permanent smile on our worthy faces (thank goodness!). Nor that life is experienced like a warm summer breeze.

When we return to our natural state of worthiness, we simply remember that, regardless of how much we weigh or what we eat (or don't), what we look like on or off Instagram, or the clumsy thing we said to that person at that time (oops), or that HUGE mistake we made (yet again), none of these things define us or make us deserving of our own cruel words and harsh punishment. None of these things diminish our fundamental goodness and value, nor lessen our belief that we have a right to respect, compassion, kindness and love. Especially our own.

A message from your future self

You know all those plates you're spinning? Don't just drop them, smash some.

Family

I awoke today, naked in my bed, with Sadness lying next to me. She was hogging the covers as she sometimes does. I got up and tried to cover her with the quilt but she followed me into the bathroom. I washed my face and looked in the mirror, and there she was, solemnly staring back at me. 'Hello,' I said. 'Welcome.' She didn't answer. She knows when I'm lying.

So I made my coffee, and Sadness joined me on the sofa. Closely followed by Gratitude. Like two loving sisters sitting either side of me as I sipped those first delicious drops. Nectar.

I felt the warmth of them both gently pressing against my body as I gazed out of the window. Sadness and Gratitude. Gratitude and Sadness. My sisters.

'Wow, I will never tire of that view of the South Downs,' whispered Gratitude. 'Nor the warmth of the sun on my face.'

'Oh, F*CK OFF,' said Sadness. And we all giggled together, as families do.

Letting go

Deep breath. Loosen your grip. Peel your fingers gently back, one by one. Say a prayer. Then dare to finally let go. Release the corpse of your old life, which you have been so desperately clinging on to. Yes, that's it; let it go.

I know you're afraid. Me too. But it's dead. Gone. Over. An empty shell. And your new life is waiting patiently to be born. So, gratefully and with deepest respect, let it go. Grieve it. Bury it. Release it.

Deep breath. New beginnings. Wobbly legs and heart.

Get on your knees. Say a prayer. Speak to a God you may not yet even believe in.

Humility. Ask for help. Listen. Then begin anew.

You're ready.

Healing

Healing offers the difference between seeing life through the eyes of your heart and responding accordingly, or looking through the blurred lens of your wounds and reacting unconsciously.

Healing the mother wound

Stage 1 – Birth mother

Understanding that no matter how wonderful (or not) our mother was/is, she still wounded us as a child (and beyond), because she was human, flawed, imperfect and perhaps even traumatised herself. Her inability to love us in the way that we needed (either by giving us too little or too much) leaves *us* with an inability to love ourselves in the way that we need. Our resistance to acknowledging her role in our suffering and struggles blocks our own capacity to heal.

Stage 2 – Inner mother

Once we have courageously grieved for all that we didn't receive from our own mother as children, we free ourselves up from her shadow and can begin to learn how to mother ourselves in healthy ways. We start to reclaim all those 'emotional orphan' parts of ourselves that have been frozen in time. We return to and for our bodies. We learn to hold healthy boundaries. We offer ourselves deep compassion, cherishing all that we are. We become the (inner) mother that we always needed and yearned for.

Stage 3 – Earth Mother

As we settle inside ourselves, letting go of all that we are not, we begin to fully remember that the ultimate mother is Mother Earth. We come to know this beyond the cognitive, as it lands deeply in our newly healed hearts. The Earth Mother is the Feminine, the giver of all Life. She nurtures, nourishes, cleanses, supports and heals us. Daily. She is the mother of our wildest dreams. Once we truly see her, truly feel her and understand her essential role, we (re)awaken and commit to doing whatever we can to save her. As if our very life depended on it.

Bang bang, you're dead

Cruel judgements are the bullets and your mouth is the gun. You can shoot yourself and/or other people but, either way, it's an act of war.

No more the warrior

If you truly want to heal and return to your wholeness, to remember once again the fullness of who you really are, then you must gratefully thank the warrior inside of you and respectfully ask her to step aside.

The warrior defence has no doubt served you very well. She is strong, driven, determined and focused. She may even have kept you alive at times. But now those days are over. You are safe and she is exhausted from being on guard 24/7.

The time has come for your warrior woman to step down from her duties and rest. This will allow the tender, soft, vulnerable and fearful part of you to breathe life again.

Healing ...

Never fear, for your warrior skills will always be available when you need them. You have honed them to perfection. You have a tenth degree black belt in defence. But the time has come to slowly and gently peel off the layers of your armour and lay down your sword, in service to the one true master.

Love.

No regrets

What's done is done. He hurt me, so I hurt you, which in turn hurts me. Cycles.

I said those words. I did that thing. It was me. Truth. Sometimes I wish I could take it all back, but that's not how it works. Reality.

The drugs, the drink, the cruel words, the selfish behaviours and poor choices. It was me. All me. Trauma.

The resistance and suffering, blame and shame, surrender and grieving. The falling and crawling. Portals.

The dark, dark nights, my bleeding heart, weary bones, ancient grief cries and the glimpse of light that follows night. Healing.

A hand to hold, unexpected laughter, tenderness, joy, kind words and warm hearts. Love's blessing.

Radical compassion, heartfelt gratitude, forgiveness, humility. Hope.

Sunrise. Beating heart. Expanse of sky. A prayer. Awakening to this new dawn. Grace.

New beginnings ...

A word to the warriors

Sometimes it's too much to do it all alone. It's just too heavy a burden to bear.

Especially when it involves your broken heart.

It's OK to ask someone to hold your hand, you know ... as long as you hold the other one.

A return to wholeness

For so much of my life I rejected the parts of me that I found lacking. The not-good-enough version, the stupid, the failure and the unlovable Donna. All the parts of me that were created in childhood, through my experiences of growing up in my family, at school and in my community.

It was as if parts of me had become frozen inside at four years old, when I first realised that I was not good enough simply being me. And at six years old, when the colour of my skin meant rejection from my (school) tribe. Then again at nine, when I struggled with maths. Stupid Donna was born as innocent Donna died. On and on it went.

All of these 'emotional orphans', which had been rejected and judged by others, were rejected and judged by me, too. I sent them packing. Banished them out into the cold, dark night. You are NOT who I am!

But of course they were (and are) all parts of my story. They were parts of who I have been and were in fact essential parts of my becoming. I was blind to this for so long. Too busy being a warrior and creating another story. One of strength, armour, defence and battle. (It was actually very lonely and exhausting but, sshh – don't tell.)

Meanwhile, the little orphan parts of me patiently waited. Cold, hungry, lonely and sad. Desperate to be invited back in. It took a long time to realise *they* were who I had been waiting for all my life. But eventually the penny dropped, I opened the door to my heart and all these mini-Donnas climbed back in. And in that moment of bliss-ful acceptance and integration of all that I am, I experienced true wholeness.

Positive anchoring

One of the simple ways for people to keep tabs on their behavioural changes is through positive anchoring. This means paying close attention each time you behave in new positive ways to 'anchor' that change inside of you, making it more likely that you will repeat it, rather than default to old negative habitual ways of being.

I invite you to get a new journal and, for a few minutes at the end of each day, review how you have overcome small (or big) challenges and take note of them, including how it felt before and after. Close your eyes and bask in each of these moments, bringing them back to life as a body memory. Noticing any physical sensations and emotions that arise as you remember what you achieved. Do this for each event, no matter how small it seems. Anchoring them inside you.

Like the moment when you dared to speak up, even though your voice was shaking. Or when you observed yourself becoming defensive, and decided instead to acknowledge the fear sitting underneath. Or perhaps it was when you dared to say, 'No,' and meant it, breaking the 'people pleaser' role and instead honouring your own boundaries.

Capture all the details of these new ways of behaving that feel more truthful, vulnerable, brave and real. More you. Write them all down with the date and descriptions, including physical sensations and the related emotions, so that you build up a little book of anchors that support you to live a more courageous, authentic and wholehearted life.

Every time you behave in new ways that feel more in alignment with who you really are and wish to be in the world, pause, notice and breathe them in. Because before long, all of these seemingly small moments of courageous living (which you previously might have skipped over) will grow into the BIG life you truly deserve.

Depression –
another perspective

Depression is about giving birth. It's about alchemy and can be the doorway to your new life. But your old one has to die first, and with it, the lies you've been told and sold. It's a painful, scary and yet necessary transformation.

Depression is also a bit like a vampire: it hides from the light and sucks the very life out of you. It only wants to wear black. So open your curtains and windows regularly, and when you do step out into the light, wear red lipstick and silver boots.

Depression is heavy to carry and so can resist movement. But every birthing mother knows she needs to move her body in order to bring new life into being. So walk, dance, stretch, breathe and shake your leaden body alive again. Dance until you sweat and roar, and tears pour down your awakening face. Let the music take you.

Creative expression is the best form of anti-depressant I know. Write, sing, sculpt, paint and draw your pain. Let the hurt bleed out of you. Create something beautiful and precious to remind you that you are alive.

Allow depression to have its way with you. Yes, you need a break from it. Yes, you need some light relief. But don't deny or resist big Mumma D. She will take you anyway. Trust in her like a birthing doula. She knows the way.

Express all of your emotions. Especially your rage. Safely. Anger will turn to passion in time, you'll see.

Head out into nature. Every day. Look at the trees, fallen leaves, wet grass; listen to the sea (she has all the answers you need); feel the wind in your hair and the rain on your face. Feel the Earth beneath your feet. Lie down, if you can. Keep looking until you can truly see. Keep connecting with the Earth until you feel something deep inside. She is the Mother you always needed and will love you back to life if you let her.

Cuddle a dog, friend or a tree. Seek help. No one should give birth alone. Tell the truth and then start to live it. And finally, I must let you know ... it's going to be a girl. Congratulations.

Judgement detox

Noticing how much we judge ourselves and/or others can be a real wake-up call. Especially for us women, with our internalised misogyny. How we 'love' to berate ourselves and our sisters, sadly. Bringing them down rather than elevating them. From what they wear, to how much they weigh and what they say or do. We judge. Breaking free from those poisoned arrows that were shot into us by the patriarchy is our work. Pulling out and snapping those insidious b*ggers one by one.

For when we are judging, there is no room for Love. Each judgement is like a window slamming shut in our heart. Sometimes, I swear, I can feel my heart shrinking when I think or say something unkind. I certainly know it hurts. And not just me. All of those unkind, harsh thoughts and words of our collective judgments become like a thick smog hanging heavy in the air, blocking every one of us from the warmth of the sun.

And what if the Joy and Peace we are all seeking are simply a life without (self) judgements? A life of understanding and compassion. Of sisterhood and inclusion. Kindness and gratitude. Can it really be that simple?

Perhaps ...

Maybe try it today. Notice how many times you go to judge yourself and others, and then stop. Flip it. Think or say something kind instead. See how that feels. A window will open in your heart. Because as judgement leaves, Joy arrives.

This much I know.

Depression –
another perspective

Your Soul wafting smelling salts under your nose.

Personal boundaries

Some boundary statements:

» No, thank you.

» That doesn't work for me.

» I don't want to do that.

» When you raise your voice like that, I stop listening.

» I haven't finished speaking, let me finish.

» That doesn't feel right for me.

» Please don't speak over me.

» If you continue to behave that way, I will leave.

» Don't speak to me that way.

» I'm not ready to share that with you.

» My appearance is none of your business.

» I need some time by myself.

» I don't know the answer to that question.

» Please don't dump your negativity in my DMs.

» I'll think about what you've said and get back to you.

» Please step back and give me some space.

» I said no.

Nope

Don't be surprised if you're met with judgement and blame when holding your boundaries with people that have none.

Sorry, not sorry

I'm a confident boundaried woman, and yet in an average day I might still say sorry five times more than I need to and four times more than I mean.

The need to apologise for absolutely everything and nothing is so ingrained in us women. It's like we are saying sorry for our very existence. If you walk into us, we say sorry. If you speak over us, we say, 'Sorry I haven't finished yet.' If we choose to say no, we often say sorry before and after we have dared to use such radical language.

Negative conditioning is so strong, as is internalised misogyny. Some women move their bodies like a walking apology. Others try to starve themselves into invisibility – 'Sorry I'm here, taking up all this space.'

Well, f*ck sorry, I say. Heartfelt apologies, yes; meaningless self-denying sorrys, no. Let's dare to break these chains of dysfunction and, in doing so, set us all free.

Not sorry, not sorry.

Learning the difference

If I say no to your request and your reaction is to get upset and angry with me, then that wasn't a request; it was a demand.

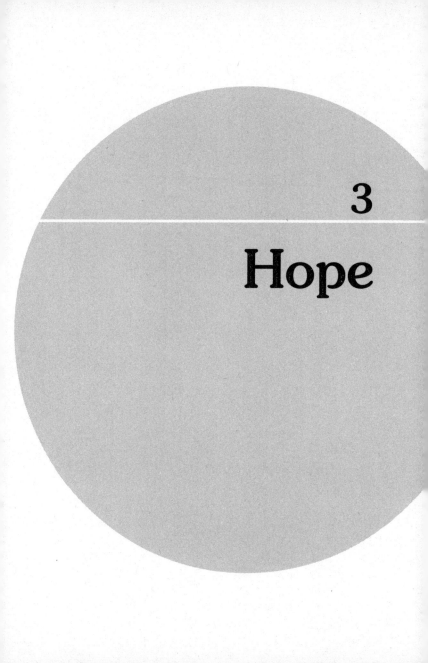

3

Hope

The lonely cloak

Sometimes I feel so lonely ... especially in a crowd. And by crowd, I mean three people or more. Including me.

It depends on the crowd, of course. But even with people I love and adore, I sometimes feel so deeply alone, trapped inside this body of mine. Like I can't quite reach them, nor them me.

I feel especially lonely when there's a need for chit-chat and polite conversation. It's like a language I don't know how to speak, so I mumble something and hope for the best. 'Yes, lovely now it's a bit cooler ...'

I feel lonely with all these screens, too. Like I'm hidden and yet seen. Do you know what I mean? I'm guessing so.

Human.

Then I head out to a different kind of crowd. The woods and forest where I live. And as I walk, carrying this heavy lonely cloak wrapped around me, I feel the trees begin to undress me. I like to imagine their branches and leaves, like arms and hands, removing this heavy garment from my back. Welcoming me home among my tribe.

And the more I walk among them, the less alone I feel.

Connected.

Then on a really blessed day, I will head out to the sea and, on entering, feel her cleansing me. Removing any residual illusion of separation. And as I lie back and float, I feel her carry me, hold me, love me. I remember that she IS me and I am her. And then I go deeper still and remember that there is no I or ME, or even WE ... only Oneness.

And I smile and weep at the beauty of it all. No longer alone after all.

Depression –
another perspective

Sometimes depression is frozen transformation, starting to defrost.

From hole to whole

When I finally had the courage to stop running and to fill the holes inside me with my unshed tears and self-compassion rather than men, substances and internalised misogyny, I found those holes became whole.

Remembering

When you see someone as full of wisdom, love and joy, what you are actually seeing is your own reflection. It's not that they have access to something that you don't. They are no more wise, loving or joyful than you are – beyond your wounds and stories. Your capacity to live like this is exactly the same as theirs. It's just that they have remembered something that you have (briefly) forgotten.

Learning to swim

When I was still holding on to a lot of emotional pain, it was as if I had a huge hole inside of me. And the devil jumped in and commanded me to dig!

So I did.

Every destructive, self-harming choice made the hole inside me bigger, wider and deeper, until it turned into a huge trench. Loyal to the cause, I dug and dug, and it rained and rained.

Until one day I lost the grip on my spade and from this exhausted, defeated place, I finally surrendered. I felt myself beginning to drown. And my body fell down, down, down into the watery silent abyss, towards rock bottom.

And down there I heard a small, clear voice whisper my name.

'Donna,' it said. 'Swim.'

So I did.

Anxiety –
a different perspective

Sometimes anxiety is simply your courage trying to find the exit door inside of you.

Alchemy

Some clues that things are working out just as they should:

» Several challenging life events happen all at once, e.g. relationship split, dog dies, you lose your job. Usually in threes.

» You start to get tired of your own dramas and stories. Even laugh at them. You stop taking yourself so seriously.

» You start to question the point of it all, the meaning of existence.

» You care less and less what others think.

» The soothers that used to numb you don't work so well anymore. Food, alcohol, weed, scrolling, whatever. It just doesn't quite cut it.

» You fall or fly ... downstairs, in the street, in your dreams, in love, off the sofa. Falling/flying becomes a theme.

» You feel very emotional. Anxiety and fears heighten. Crying lots spontaneously and seemingly for nothing.

» Anger starts to surface ... Things that didn't use to bother you really piss you off.

» You have a strong pull to be around deeper and wiser people. Shallow MFs have to be released. You let go of out-of-date relationships, including the old negative one with yourself.

» You start to want to help others, not as a martyr, but for the sheer hell of it. You become kinder, softer, more tender.

» You need more time alone. You feel separate and connected.

» You start to collect things from the natural world: leaves, conkers, pebbles, shells. The magpie in you is set free.

» Your laugh sounds more like a cackle (this last one is a joke ... she cackles ...).

Open up

Sometimes anxiety is simply truth without a voice.

Clueless

Every deepening person reaches a point in their life when they believe they are absolutely clueless about themselves and life itself. They look in the mirror and have no idea who is staring back at them. 'Who the hell am I!?' they ask no one in particular. 'What's my purpose? How do I find meaning?'

Not a clue.

'Why do I still feel this way? Will this sadness ever end? And how on earth do I find my way back?'

Not a clue.

'What should I do with my life?'

'What are my next steps?'

'Is there really a deeper meaning to it all?'

'What the hell is going on in this world ... ?!'

... *Tumbleweed* ...

This not-knowing phase is a painful but necessary part of deepening into life. It is essential to become absolutely lost as to who we are and what the hell is going on. To become certain about only one thing, which is how little we know about anything at all.

The ego will of course put up a good fight. Fists at the ready. It will still try to control (*bless*), desperate to make sense of it all, to manipulate and speed up the process one way or another. (Good luck with that.)

Until eventually, we, the clueless, have the sense to lower our flailing fists, remove the gloves (defence) and simply surrender to the not-knowing. To say to ourselves first and then out loud, 'I have absolutely no clue who I am, what I'm doing or where I'm going.'

And then, just like that, as if by magic, a door quietly swings open ...

A bitter pill

What if some forms of depression are not really sickness, but instead the medicine we actually need? A nasty-tasting course of treatment, prescribed for us by the Universe, that forces us to stop running long enough to grieve, heal, grow, deepen and awaken?

And what if Love is the only cure?

Imagine this.

Depression –
another perspective

Your Soul giving you the kiss of Life.

Spring-clean

You can't get to the new without giving up the old. Whether that's outdated behaviours, relationships, conditioned negative beliefs, ancient fears or self-sabotaging choices.

It's a universal law that we must discard something old to make space for something new to arrive. So who or what are you willing to let go of in the pursuit of your own dreams?

Look again

You are waiting for a miracle ... but YOU are the miracle. Everything else is just a lie you've been sold. And the world needs more miracles.

Seasons

At some point, all of us will find ourselves stumbling around in yet another dark and cold season of our lives. Often we try to resist it and are taken anyway, kicking and screaming, down into the depths of a winter phase. It seems we forget how to trust the darkness and to have faith in the wisdom of the seasons.

Some of us will even try to carry on in denial of the cold and bitter winds arriving in our life, or the heavy, dark clouds hanging over our heads. A bit like continuing to wear your flip-flops and summer dress in a snowstorm. Useless and bloody freezing!

Because what we really need in these frozen winter phases of life is warmth. Warm heart, warm words, warm tears, warm friends, warm hugs, warm therapist, cosy home and bed. A warm hand to hold. The perfect ingredients to support us as we grow underground during the cold, harsh seasons of our life.

For each of us it's about having the courage to turn towards the dark winter, surrendering to it and asking for its message. 'What is it that you have come to teach me?' Then stop running (in your flip-flops) long enough to hear the darkness whisper its answer.

An awakening life will always involve periods in the dark, you know. Seasons. It's the deal we make with the Universe when we begin to wake up from our restless slumber.

And then one (extra)ordinary day, when the dark winter within us has completed its sacred mission, it will quietly leave. Give humble thanks. Then head out into nature with a grateful heart and open eyes. Look down and you will see there, peeking up through the frosty ground, a new precious bud. Look up and you will see a small yet radiant glimmer of light peeking through between the dark clouds.

Spring is on the way.

Move towards it ...

Living courageously

Just because someone is good at certain things in life, it doesn't mean that they come easy to them. I know lots of introverts and sensitive types who work in what you might call an extroverted field, like activism, public speaking, TV presenting or group facilitation. Despite their natural need for privacy, solitude and one-to-one connections, their job (purpose?) requires them to communicate and mix with large numbers of people. In doing so they face internal challenges every time they need to leave their cave and step out into the bright, loud lights of this extroverted world.

That's courageous living.

I include myself in this. I've been working with people and leading groups for over 30 years now and I'm pretty good at it. But that doesn't mean it comes easily. I still get nervous every single time I do a group Zoom session or lead a workshop or speak at an event for the first time. I still need lengthy recovery time afterwards, in my cave, following a big exposure to people. Being around large groups drains my energy, even though I LOVE people with my whole heart. I have learned the hard way to take enough time to rest and recharge afterwards. Consciously releasing their stories and pain from my body, and particularly from my heart. They are not mine to carry.

I've also come to view my nerves as a more positive experience over time. I often say that excitement and nerves are close siblings. Those nerves remind me that I'm very much alive. They show me that even after all these years, I still care about people and what I do. And the truth is, there is still a part of me that is a shy, vulnerable and innocent five-year-old girl peeking out from behind her mummy's skirt, wanting to be liked and to belong. And that to me is nothing short of a beautiful miracle.

Maybe

Maybe happiness is simply a life without (self) judgement ...

Both/and

When your heart breaks, it also opens. That's a painful and yet beautiful truth.

Many times in life, as we face the sorrows and darkness, we can (understandably) forget to notice that light and beauty still exist. It's not either/or but both/and. This wisdom alone will save us.

Our relationship is over, we get really sick or the love of our life dies, and our heart shatters into a million tiny pieces ...

... And yet look down there, among the shards, and you will see a tiny purple flower growing up through the concrete. She waves at you like an old friend. Tenacious and fragile. Just like you.

Both/and.

Then over time and after space to grieve, life begins to feel like summer again. Blissss.

And then ...

... Another heartbreak arrives to bring you to your knees. Nose down once again in Humility Street you go.

Yet, even as you're face down there in the dirt, you will notice how the sun still shines its warmth on your back, and you will feel the tender touch of an angel's hand offering to help you get back up.

Both/and.

Every heartbreak can be soothed by noticing this. That even in our darkest hours, Love never leaves us. Perhaps especially then. She will show us this exquisite truth.

And as you stagger back up to your feet, you will hear an ice-cream van coming around the corner. Reminding you that it's still summer and there's still ice cream to be eaten.

So lift up your weary head, and gently carry your broken open heart towards that beautiful sound of summer.

Both/and.

The uninvited guest

Pain is the greatest spiritual teacher, I know. It teaches us what it means to truly Live and Love. It makes us tender, vulnerable, wiser, more open and humble. If we let it.

Pain always arrives like an uninvited guest banging on your door late at night, demanding to be let in. Awakening you from your cosy slumber. It sweeps in and 'requests' that you unpack its luggage. So rude.

You can try to ignore it, but pain will only stay longer if you do. So you resentfully lift up its heavy bag and start to unpack. Inside Pain's luggage is all of your grief, hidden among the wine bottles, work diary, biscuits and mobile phone.

As you dig deep into this Mary Poppins bag of pain, you will find yourself at ten years old, when your father left. Deeper still and there's seven-year-old bullied you standing alone, crying in the playground. And what's that hidden behind the spoonful of sugar? Oh yes, that's the 35-year-old you whose marriage fell apart.

And as you continue to rummage inside pain's luggage, you discover emotions long denied, related to those heartbroken parts of yourself. Like rage and fear, hopelessness and despair. You look inside the empty wine bottle, desperate for some relief, and discover only teardrops left at the bottom. So instead you allow the pain to speak, and you scream and shout, write, roar, shake and dance it out of you. To your utmost surprise, you start to cry the tears of the living.

On and on it goes, and just as you feel that pain will never leave, she stands up and smiles at you and slowly makes her way to the door. So bloody graceful. Finally, she is ready to leave, and places a gift in your hands as she exits. You look down and notice it has a turd for a bow and you can't help but smile. You carefully open Pain's parting gift and there, inside, is an empty box. And engraved on the bottom are four simple letters.

HOPE.

You place this hard-won gift carefully into your heart and then open the curtains to let the light in. You take a shower to cleanse body and Soul. And as the blissful cool water falls upon your weary skin, you say a prayer of deep gratitude and begin to giggle ...

4

Relationships

A friendship vow

I've recently made a new friend and so have updated my 'friendship vows'. I wrote these because in the past I have hurt people with my mixed messages. As an introvert, I like both connection and space, intimacy and privacy. So now I have begun to clarify my friendship boundaries from the start of a new 'friendship romance'. This might sound clinical, especially to the unboundaried! But I simply don't want to hurt anyone, and I'm too old to say yes and not mean it.

» Emotional honesty – I vow to be honest about my feelings and if I get triggered. I will aim to respond (not react) in any disagreements we may encounter. I welcome them, rather than run from them, as I know these only deepen connection.

» Acceptance – I commit to accepting all that you are and ask for the same in return. I will share my light and shadow. Sometimes that means some ugly sh*t will bubble up. I don't expect you to like it, but I do ask that you accept it. Including the smell. I will do the same for you.

» Differences – we are two different people and I welcome that. I will be curious about your choices and welcome our differences. (Including coffee choices.)

» Connecting – I commit to investing in our relationship. I don't expect you to always be available nor answer my messages within an 'appropriate' timescale. As an introvert, less is more for me. I don't need to see you often, but you will always be with me.

» Needs – I vow not to have unrealistic expectations of you. You are not my parent, so I don't expect you to parent me! If I need something, I will ask. I'm OK with a yes or a no.

» Truth – I will do my best to tell you the truth. Sometimes I might tell a small lie if I'm feeling vulnerable. When back in my wisdom, I will share with you why I felt the need to be dishonest in that moment.

» Apology – I will apologise when I make a mistake and take responsibility for any clumsy actions or words. (There will be a few.)

» Laughter – I will laugh with you and at you. Please do me the honour of doing the same! My humour will sometimes be dark but always kind. Yours doesn't have to be. As long as you're funny. If you're not funny, I won't laugh.

Relationships

For almost ten years I worked mainly with couples, and here are a few things I learned along the way (which may or may not be true):

» Opposites might attract but they will also eventually irritate.

» You can't make someone love you.

» Apart from parents and kids, your (ex) partner will be the greatest spiritual teacher you will ever learn from.

» Attachment and love are two very different things.

» If your parents' relationship was dysfunctional, you will need to learn how to healthily relate.

» Hurt people hurt people.

» If you can give love but not receive it, you do not know true intimacy.

» Love is not transactional.

» True love doesn't end just because the relationship does.

» Neediness and connection are not the same thing.

» It's not possible to have a healthy relationship with a partner who behaves like an emotional child. It just means you end up becoming their parent.

» Love addiction is as powerful as any drug I know.

» People can spend their whole relationship transferring their parent(s) over the top of their partner, so in fact never truly seeing or knowing who is really there.

» Romantic love is a phase. Enjoy it, cultivate it even, but it's not meant to consistently last. That's just in fairy tales.

» We are often drawn to partners that remind us (and sometimes even look like) our parents ... for better and worse.

» Projection is reflection. Same, same.

» Couples don't need to sleep in the same bed ... unless they actually want to!

» So many couples marry without questioning why ...

» Monogamy is a tough ask for most – 50-plus years of enjoying sex with the same person. Now that's a challenge!

» Sometimes people hurt those they love ... Good people can make poor choices. That's real life.

» If you don't argue and resolve issues, watch the passion and sex drain from your relationship, and the resentment grow.

» Although annoying, the argument is never really about the loo seat being left up.

Best friends forever

My body is like a best friend that I fell out with many years ago. We lost touch for a while. I ignored her for years (although she never stopped calling). Eventually, I realised it was up to me to make the first move and apologise for all my harsh judgements, all my rejections of her. Luckily, she's the forgiving type.

It feels so good to reconnect with my body. To love and accept her just as she is (as BFFs do). I didn't realise how much I had missed her until I saw her again through the eyes of my heart.

When we shift from viewing our body as an object for others' pleasure (or our own displeasure) to seeing it as the life-sustaining miracle it actually is, everything in our life will begin to change. Everything.

Growing up

When you have a relationship with someone – anyone, actually: a friend, partner, family member, colleague or even a person on the street – it's important to ask yourself what part of them you are relating to, at any given moment. Is it their wise adult self that you are communicating with? Or is it their wounded-child aspect? It is especially important to know the answer when there's any kind of disagreement or conflict between you, because if you are triggered back into your five-year-old self and want to protect that vulnerable part of you, and they are also coming from their defended five-year-old self, then two little kids are essentially trying to resolve a 'grown-up' situation. This rarely ends well.

If you have already done any kind of personal development work, then (I hate to break it to you) you need to take responsibility and be the one who takes the lead in trying to communicate from an adult place. This doesn't mean you won't get triggered, it doesn't mean you can't have the odd tantrum, but it does mean that you will be the first to lead the way with generous apologies. You will initiate a different kind of conversation. It means you will endeavour to connect to and from your heart, even though it's hidden beneath all the layers of your defences, and authentically and courageously reconnect with this person (aged five) standing in front of you.

Sometimes this involves what I call 'saying the unsayable', whereby you dig deep inside and – ignoring the ego's demands to win or *be right* – you tell them what's in your heart. 'I know I reacted like a five-year-old just now and I apologise. What I said was unkind and I didn't mean it. I'm just afraid. Can we start again, please?'

Watch your world (and *the* world) transform with that kind of honest and courageous communication. Your five-year-old self will be so proud.

5

Gratitude and Joy

Love's Face

When a new day dawns and light peeks in through your bedroom window, know that this is Love landing upon your awakening face. Welcoming you into this extra day that you have been gifted. So say thank you.

When the sun shines its smile upon your weary bones, know that you are being bathed and held in the warmth of Divine Love. Say thank you.

When the wind and rain pour down upon your sleepy face, and the storm batters you awake once again. Feel yourself being cleansed by Love's Grace. You may groan and moan, resist then surrender. But always, always, say thank you.

As you breathe in the air, without effort, feel Love gifting you life-force, nourishing your whole body continuously, asking nothing of you in return. So say thank you.

As you stand up and walk upon the solid earth, feel yourself held in Love's Grace. Weep with joy, sing and dance your thank-yous.

This is the secret beauty we can all miss. Love's Face. This is the Love you long for. Right here, right now, as you read this, Life is Loving you. So don't miss it. Feel it. Know it. Believe it. Then get down on your knees and weep with gratitude. Let your life be your thank you.

Gratitude loon

Here's a simple practice that will change your life.

When you wake up and before you even leave your bed, place your hand on your heart and feel it beating beneath your chest, and then say thank you. Speak these magical words (which are also a prayer) out loud. Regardless of the circumstances of your life, any illness or extra weight you might be carrying, you are alive and your body is a miracle. As are you. So say thank you.

Speaking of miracles ... spend a few moments more looking at your body, like you would a new lover, and say thank you to each part. To your feet for walking you around, your funny little toes for keeping your balance, your strong legs for holding you up, your stomach for putting up with your judgements, your gut for digesting your food, etc. Offer each part of you a warm, loving welcome into this new day that you have been gifted. Say thank you to each and, most importantly, mean it. (You can also do this in the shower, if you're in a hurry.)

Then carry this gratitude around with you into your day. (Write it on your hand/a Post-it if you need a reminder.) From your first morning wee to that amazing coffee and the colour of the sky. Speak your thanks out loud to the view from your window, to the flowers and the trees, and to your family and friends. Dare to look and sound like a gratitude loon!

Because when you let this depth of appreciation land in your heart, it will change your life completely.

Try it if you don't believe me.

You can even begin right now.

A recipe for joy

Here's my simple recipe for cultivating more joy in your life.

Ingredients:

» Making time for simple activities that relax and de-stress you, so that your joy can flow – walking, cooking, reading, meditating and spending time with family, friends, pets, trees ... whatever floats your boat and doesn't involve a screen.

» Expressing yourself creatively – singing, dancing, painting, drawing, decorating, gardening, doing whatever fills your heart.

» Scheduling time for laughter, fun and play. Life can feel serious enough, so dedicate time to lightening your load. Add a dollop of belly laughs and silliness for good measure. Laughing at yourself is particularly tasty.

» Investing in relationships that activate your joy. Recycling or discarding those that are past their sell-by date.

» Being in service – finding ways to support others and connect meaningfully with your community.

» Moving your body. Joy is energy, and movement allows this energy to flow. Get up and get moving. Shake and dance your way towards more joy.

Stir together and sprinkle on top a generous amount of Love, kindness and appreciation. Yum.

You know those recipes with a special ingredient that makes the difference between tasty and absolutely delicious? Like that small piece of dark chocolate you add to a chilli? Well, that magic ingredient for this recipe is *gratitude*. Focus your attention on all that you have to be grateful for (without denying any struggles you are facing) and watch your joy rise, like a perfect soufflé.

Joy is an internal celebration. A way of being that requires regular practice. It's also highly contagious, with a ripple effect that flows far and wide. So make sure you share your delicious dish of joy with many different people, because the more you invest in spreading your joy, the more delicious your life will taste.

A date with wonder

A date with wonder = a conscious period of time spent looking at the natural environment as if seeing it all for the very first (or last) time.

A date with wonder isn't only about cultivating gratitude and joy. It's also about reconnecting you to yourself, to your own body and in turn to the body of the Earth. For to fully embody our spirit, we must always return to the nature that we are a part of – bask in its beauty, bathe in its wonders and let it guide us and wash us clean; reminding us of our place in the family of things. Until eventually we remember that we are living and breathing with all Life as one.

If you string enough of these dates with wonder together, pretty soon you will find that you're having one long, deep love affair with Life.

Fields of joy

Plant enough seeds of gratitude deep in your heart and water them daily, then watch how flowers called joy begin to bloom.

The Joy revolution

Joy is radical activism. And Joy's middle name is Love. To live joyfully is to transform the world. A Joy activist has the power to touch and transform anyone and everyone, without even needing to meet them. Her joyful energy emanates out into the world like a prayer, spreading far and wide. It lands like a tender loving kiss upon the bruised hearts of the sleeping wounded.

'You are seen,' Joy whispers. 'And you are Loved.'

When there are enough Joy activists out there weaving their magic, sprinkling their Joy dust, anything and everything is possible. They are secretly healing the world – one smile, one giggle, one song and one dance at a time. Come join the Revolution.

Joy is what arrives as expectation leaves.

6

Authentic

Authenticity

Authenticity is a word that gets used a lot, but what does it actually mean? We know the dictionary definition but here's what it means to me.

Authenticity is essentially about truth. It's about getting real. We often need to do this with ourselves first, before we are ready to share this truth with others.

Getting real is about daring to peel back the false layers and masks one by one, and discover the person you really are that's buried underneath. That's the truth of you. The one that existed before the world broke your heart one too many times.

Authenticity is about stumbling and bumbling, it's about getting back up after the fall, with a wonky smile and dirt on your nose, and saying 'whoopsie'.

It's about vulnerability and courage, the not knowing and the no. It's about daring to live the bigger life you were meant to live before the (toxic) world convinced you otherwise. It's about that yes.

It's about shining so brightly that the world needs its sunglasses just to look at you. Sunscreen is also a good idea. And the sad truth is that not everyone likes bright light ... Some prefer to stay in the shade.

And finally, authenticity is about shining AND taking your flaws along with you for the ride. Not as an unwelcome guest, but as a bunch of invited besties strapped in alongside you on the roller-coaster of your life.

Now, that's authenticity with her best knickers on.

Enjoy the ride.

Living authentically

It's not that it doesn't scare me sometimes to speak my truth ... it's just that it scares me much more to live a lie.

Vulnerability

Here are some vulnerability statements – some that I've heard from others and some I've dared to say ...

»   I'm looking to make new friends. Can we meet for a coffee sometime?

»   Will you come with me? I don't want to go by myself.

»   I always get nervous when I meet new people.

»   I'm so sorry, I was wrong to say/do that.

»   Please will you stay longer? I feel lonely.

»   I said that to try to impress you, but it's not actually true.

»   I was really hurt by what you said.

»   My heart is broken.

»   I love you.

»   I don't find that funny.

»   I'm leaving you to find myself.

»   I don't agree with what you're saying.

»   What's on my Instagram page is not the full picture.

»   I can't go on like this.

»   I'm scared you won't like the true me.

»   Deep down inside I worry I'm not a very nice person.

»   Can I have a hug, please?

» Sometimes it feels like you don't like me.

» I don't know what to say.

» I miss touch.

» I'm scared you're going to hurt me.

» Can you tell me something you like about me?

» No.

Rise up

When women start to wake up and return to the truth of who they are, there is often a lot of anger, impatience and irritation that needs to rise from inside of them and clear away. Suddenly, you will find yourself shifting from smiling sweetly and nodding quietly as someone speaks over you (yet again) to saying loudly, 'I haven't finished speaking!' or even, 'Wait your turn.' (*I know!!*)

Don't worry, you're not turning into a terrible monster – though some still-sleeping folks might try to say otherwise. ('I preferred you before.'; 'You're so aggressive now.') You are simply allowing all those decades of suppressed frustrations and swallowed truths start to surface ... and you're just too damn tired to wrap them up in a sugar-coated package, in order to make it easier for others to swallow. 'Find your own sugar, I'm busy.'

So you will find yourself saying stuff like, 'Oh god, no!' or, 'That doesn't work for me,' and 'I'm not available then.' (With no explanation whatsoever. Eek.) Your power starts to flood through you and your body with an almighty ROAR. 'I said, no.'; 'I'm speaking, let me finish,' and of course the good old, 'F*ck you!' It's as if a lifetime's worth of truth just tumbles out of you. It can't and won't be stopped. It isn't comfortable but it's absolutely necessary.

And as the rage begins to settle, and you find your stride with this new power and truth that is (and has always been) you, you feel your female lineage walking behind you, inside you and through you. No more hiding, no more lying. No more shrinking. Only wonderful, powerful, truthful, naked you.

Commitment

Sometimes my body gains weight, especially when it feels unsafe. Sometimes it speaks to me in a language I don't understand. Lately it heats up to let me know when I'm stressed or lying. It's a truth-seeking wonder!

It's been abused, violated, deprived, neglected, starved and stuffed. It's been judged, criticised, compared, punished and denied. And yet still it loves me enough to stay alive, healthy and whole. How amazing is that?!

So when I look in the mirror nowadays, I see a beautiful gift, a miracle. A body full of curves and softness and trauma scars and Love. A body with a fabulous story to tell.

And through all the years of punishment, and the cruel harsh words it has received from me and others, it has never once betrayed me, always had my best interests at heart. Even when it gets sick, I know it's to make me stop and rest. I'm so grateful. This body carries my Soul, my heart, my hopes and my longings. It allows me to feel the tender touches of my grandsons. The sun on my face. The taste of ice cream.

And finally, now I can love my body. In fact, I refuse not to. And I will not betray it another single day with a harsh judgement or by giving it away to someone who does not cherish it the way I do.

Authentic

As I began to change and grow, becoming more myself once again, I noticed that many people preferred the old version of me. The 'give herself away, jokey, unboundaried, love everyone but herself' Donna suited them much better (thank you very much). But it didn't suit me.

One day I woke up and I just couldn't wear any more masks. There were so many options scattered across my bedroom floor and they had all become so incredibly heavy. Confusing, too, playing all those different roles. 'Who on earth am I going to be today!?'

I reached a point where I couldn't pretend for another single moment to be anything other than flawed, imperfect, fabulous me. It was scary, though, at first. When I took that final mask off and looked in the mirror, I couldn't see anything at all. It was as if I'd disappeared, which I guess was sort of true. But slowly, as I began to live and speak more honestly and authentically, my face reappeared with its new shape, as I returned to the truth of me.

It's not always easy to be real, you know. Sometimes it seems much easier to slap on a 'fake-it face' (FIF!). It takes a lot of courage to show up just as I am. Nothing more, nothing less. Sometimes, being true to myself means that someone else is left feeling disappointed. Sometimes, when I speak my truth, it might not be what another person wants to hear. And I'm becoming more and more OK with that. Because that's the reality of authentic living.

And ultimately, what it brings me is the most incredible sense of comfort and ease in this imperfect and true skin, as I bumble and stumble and gratefully grow through this terrifying and beautiful experience called Life.

And nowadays, when I look in the mirror, I really like what I see. Me.

Hot stuff

Anger and Passion are like close family members. Twins even. They belong to one another.

Often, as women, we will suppress and deny our anger, swallowing our frustrations along with our truth, and find over time that our mojo has made a swift exit. We no longer seem able to access our passion for life, and our whole energy system becomes exhausted, stagnant and dull without it.

We notice this lack of passion rippling across all areas of our life, including our sex drive. All that undigested rage sitting in our gut, blocking our sexual energy and the very life-force that sits beneath it.

So if you're wondering where your mojo has gone and why you hardly ever fancy a good old romp anymore, you might want to take a look at where you last left your anger.

Because once you safely begin to access and release this anger, through your body and your voice, you might just reignite the fire inside you, and discover that your va-va-voom starts to return and burn.

Truth

The moment we begin to tell the Truth is the moment everything begins to change. Nothing in our life can remain the same, once Truth has shown her face.

Truth comes in many forms: she shows up in the words we say and those we don't. She speaks loudly in what we do and even louder in what we don't. All of our emotions are pure Truth. Our tears are in fact little droplets of liquid Truth. And expressing our grief is one of the most truthful ways we will ever show up in the world.

The body itself always speaks Truth. It's the only language it knows. Not sure what to do or say? Ask your body and then listen …

Sometimes our Truth is about acknowledging to ourselves how we are living a lie. We may not be ready to change that lie yet, but calling it what it is, even to ourselves – now, that's Truth.

Truth can be challenging, painful, life-shattering and terrifying. That's true. It is also cleansing, courageous, heart-opening and liberating.

Dare to tell the Truth.

It really will set you free.

The truth teller

Truth is admitting when you're lying to yourself.

Truth is when you dare to say you haven't got a clue what the hell you're doing.

Truth is about holding boundaries, even when it makes your bum clench and your armpits sweat with fear.

Truth says, 'I choose me.'

Truth is no.

Truth is nuanced. It's not interested in facts or black and white. It's comfortable in the grey (although it's really more silver ...).

Truth speaks in tears, rage, grief and great whoops of joy.

The body speaks truth even when the words will not come. And the eyes tell only the truth. Always.

The truth is I don't know.

Truth says, 'I Love you,' or 'I don't love you anymore.'

Truth says, 'I'm too scared to leave.'

Truth will leave when it's time.

Truth says, 'I'm terrified, but I just can't do this anymore.'

Truth says, 'I'm lonely, please hold me. Help.'

Truth is dancing and singing without fear of being judged. Truth doesn't mind what wounds others might see.

Truth hates to wear a bra.

Truth loves silver and glitter the most.

Truth is yes.

Truth is first felt, then written, then spoken, then lived.

Absence of truth is a lonely place.

Truth is a compass.

Truth is home.

Truth says, 'I know there's something more ...'

Truth looks down first and then up.

Truth is sacred. A celebration. It's a glitter ball.

Truth is where the light gets in.

7

Love with a Capital L

The seven stages
for returning to Love

In the beginning there is only Love. The one with a capital L. And then as the human experience truly unfolds, we start to forget.

Here are the key stages:

1. Pain – first comes the pain ... the separation, rejection, abandonment and loss. Heartbreak. The denial of which causes more suffering than the original wound. Ouch.

2. Healing – next there is the healing phase, slowly, deeply, courageously turning towards that which aches and breaks. Grieving all that we have lost. Applying love to fill up all those holes inside.

3. Unlearning – then comes the crucial phase of unlearning ... breaking all of the negative patterns, loyalties and dysfunctional belief systems that have been passed down blindly through your family lineage. Cutting the negative cords that bind you to the past.

4. Learning – next comes learning ... or rather, re-learning. Remembering the innocence, truth, loving kindness and playfulness of your childhood, whilst being led by the wisdom and deep Love of your own Soul. This takes humility, curiosity, vulnerability and surrender. It leads to radical joy.

5. Awakening – eventually we arrive at full awakening ... if only for a moment. An opening of the eye(s) to all of the egoic stories from the past, and the illusion of separation and 'otherness'. Here we remember the oneness and miracle of it all. We

recognise our very life as Grace and surrender to Life itself, with complete and utter Faith in the uncertainty, chaos, pain and exquisite beauty of it all.

6. Deeper still – we start to regularly weep with gratitude and joy, as we recognise that our time in human form is fleeting. It will be over soon. Maybe today, tomorrow, in 30 years ... who knows? It's quick. In facing the end, we can truly begin. No time to waste.

7. Love beyond love – we see beyond the illusion of love as something to give, receive, lose or earn, and remember it as who and what we are. We return to where we began. To Love with a capital L. And here we look back to see those walking behind us and reach out a hand to guide them onwards.

'This way, all is well, follow the trail ...'

Love is the medicine

Love has never hurt you. And she never will. Nothing hurtful, painful or cruel was ever acted out in the name of True Love.

Nothing.

Attachment, desire, control, rage, need and disconnection perhaps. Yes. Some even masquerading as love (with a little l). But never Love itself.

Because True Love never harms, she only heals. And it's true that True Love never dies. Even when the person does. Or when they leave. Love remains behind.

Always.

This kind of Love (the only real kind) lives on and on. For it was never ours to give or to receive. It is only for us to remember its taste. This Love is our true nature and birthright. She is the medicine to all dis-ease. The antidote to all Soul sickness and suffering. The warm light of summer after the long, dark winter.

If we let her, Love will comfort, heal and save us all.

Kindness = love in action

Kindness is a word, a look, a touch, a behaviour, a possibility.

Kindness is the language of the heart and is universal.

It is spoken by everyone, if they dare to let their heart speak.

Kindness is hope.

Kindness is a reaching forwards, towards; a hand to hold, an arm to lean on, a tender touch. Kindness is a moment, a presence, a smile, warm eyes and listening ears.

Kindness reminds you that you matter. That you are seen, heard and understood. It shows you that you are loved.

Kindness whispers in your ear tales of reassurance, love and freedom.

Kindness doesn't judge. It understands. You made mistakes. Me too.

Kindness makes you question if there's more to life than the horrors in your head. It makes your heart ache and your tears fall. In a good way, which is the only way.

Kindness says, 'Step back from the edge. Climb down from that ledge. Take my hand.' Kindness beckons you to stay a while longer. Long enough to allow its medicine to heal you. Kindness says, 'I love you, I've got you. I'm here.'

Kindness asks you, 'Please will you stay? Don't leave. There's more ...'

Kindness is love in action.

So love more. Reach for.

Be kind. Always.

In love

When we speak of self-love, we know that it's an inside job but when we think of 'being Loved', we typically think of others, outside of ourselves, offering this love to us. A lover, a friend, a pet, a partner, a family member. Someone 'out there' who will love us into being.

And yet the truth of it is, we are being Loved every single moment of every single day. We are never not being Loved. Even (perhaps especially) in our darkest hours and loneliest nights. Even within the chaos and craziness of life's storms, even hidden beneath the fears and self-loathing. Yes, even then, we are Loved. The sky loves us. The stars and the moon, too. The birds, the trees, the flowers, the sea, the air we breathe. The land we walk upon. Even the raindrops are liquid love. The food we eat, the water we drink and bathe in ... I could go on and on! So. Much. Love.

Mother Earth is loving us every moment and, as with our own mothers, even when we don't deserve it, she just goes ahead and loves us anyway. Just as with our own mothers, we are blind to her sacrifices. We take them all for granted, not even noticing how she gives everything of herself to us. Always.

True love.

So open your eyes, lift up your weary head and breathe in this abundance of love. Let it fill you and land in your very bones. Breathe out only 'thank you'. And eventually, one day you will drop down to your knees, weeping with gratitude at the deepest realisation that you are love(d). You are love(d). You are love(d).

Where love lives

It was a tough day when I finally realised that no one was coming to save me. In truth, I still sometimes (usually at night) fantasise that they will. But at least these days I know it's a fantasy and enjoy it for what it is, a brief flirtation with a fairy tale.

It was a BIG life-shifting moment when I realised that I had become addicted to misery. That in wearing only my sh*t goggles each day, unsurprisingly, it was all I ever saw. EVERYWHERE. And in truth, it was all I really knew. Yes, my life felt like sh*t, but it was safer to wallow in that stench than to go about the tough, painful job of climbing out and cleaning up my act.

It was a reluctant day when I realised that no one was to blame for my life, including me. That it wasn't about blame anymore, or remaining a victim, but just about healing and making new choices. Better, kinder, more loving ones. Over time these small, yet powerful, choices grew into my new life. Simple but not easy.

It was an (extra)ordinary day when I realised that my present and my future were no longer defined by my past. That all the hard inner work had been worth it. That's when I really woke up. All three eyes wide open. And now every morning I pop on my triple-lens gratitude goggles, and guess what? I find Love lives everywhere. Even in the dirt. I see it, I feel it, I know it, I live it. I am it. (As are you.)

Purpose

People often speak of a need to 'find their purpose', and yet your purpose is exactly the same as mine, as everyone's. And that is simply to remember that you are Love. That you have never not been Love, and you will never be anything other than Love.

Once you come to deeply know (remember) this, your only purpose then is to live, breathe and *be* this Love in the world. Because as you emanate Love out into the wider world, others will feel your Love land inside them and will begin to slowly remember their own. What better purpose can there possibly be than this?

Love's paradox

To love and accept yourself, even when you continue to self-sabotage and behave in ways that do not reflect how loveable and precious you really are – now, that's true commitment. That's radical self-love right there.

LOVE beyond love

I choose to believe that when I pray for someone, I am energetically sending beams of Love into their heart. A bit like sharing my favourite chocolates with them, regardless of whether I believe they 'deserve' it.

Every time I pray for someone, I am imagining Love from my heart travelling across the world to wherever they are and secretly landing inside their heart, as they sleep or scroll, snap at their kids, cry, take their meds, or even make really bad choices that harm others. (Those people might even get two chocolates – they clearly need extra.)

This kind of prayer has nothing to do with God or religion and everything to do with pure unconditional Love. Love with a capital L.

Now some of you may find this idea rather silly and roll your eyes as you read this. And I don't mind, because I am still going to sneak my last Rolo into your heart regardless. That's how much I Love you.

Making Love

Spreading kindness like confetti, she slowly makes love to the whole world.

8

Wisdom

This

What if this is it?

What if there is no better place for you to be, no ultimate nirvana for you to reach? Knowing that it isn't the circumstances of your life that need 'fixing', just your lenses.

Perspective.

What if you have been hanging out in heaven all along?

What if you are mistaken, thinking that you are in any way broken or flawed, and in fact there's nothing wrong with you? What if you do not have anything missing but are simply missing something ...

And that is remembering who and what you really are.

A child of the Universe.

A shining star.

What if the journey really is the destination? A cliché that is true nevertheless.

That right here, right now, contains everything you will ever need.

And every stumble and bumble was only ever sent to make you humble (!).

Becoming more grateful, tender and loving as you fall. That is all.

TIMBERRRRRRR! And there she goes again. Face down in the dirt of Humility Street.

Nirvana.

What if your life is filled with invisible grace in every single breath you take?

Yes, even (especially) down there in the dirt.

You are still breathing, in and out, grace.

What if?

Truth detectives

One of the biggest lies us women are sold by the patriarchy is that there is something wrong with us. That we are fundamentally flawed from birth and that if only we were sweeter, prettier, slimmer, curvier, more 'feminine', more intelligent (not too much!), less emotional, younger, quieter, more rational, etc. perhaps Big Daddy P would finally love and accept us.

Instead, he feeds on all the seeds of insecurities he planted inside us before we'd even had the opportunity to learn that most power-full word: 'NO'. Cultivating our insecurities day in and out, until we forget who we really are and what we are capable of. Like one enormous cloak of amnesia wrapped around our 'inadequate' bodies and minds. So that we start to live as if we are 'less than', and to use patriarchal language against ourselves and our sisters. This robs us all of our worth, our power, our wisdom and our very essence.

And then, in order to cope with these insidious lies seeping into our Souls, we have to buy stuff, drink stuff, eat stuff, snort stuff ('not very ladylike'!) and self-medicate with our drugs of 'choice'. All part of the master plan so that we continue to feed the consumerist, materialist and capitalist machine that is the big sweaty balls and c*ck of the patriarchy.

Our job as women is to (re)awaken. To become truth detectives in our own lives and in Life itself. To begin to forensically sift out the lies we have been told and sold from the very beginning. To dare to speak out (what we have always known) ... that the Emperor is buck naked.

As we (re)awaken and begin to consciously fall back in love with ourselves, we can view this work for what it is – the most powerful activism we will ever undertake. For to love yourself completely is to remember and honour your own Soul. To love yourself completely is to love and honour all girls and women. To accept all parts of you as more than enough is to reclaim your sacred feminine power – by word, by deed, by crown, by choice.

And from here, anything and everything becomes possible.

The world (including our precious boys and gentle-men) needs you to remember this. It's time to wake up.

Two steps forwards

If we never go backwards, in our efforts to move forwards, how will we get to meet all those old parts of ourselves, to say hello and welcome them home?

When I've stumbled backwards, it's often been forwards. All at the same time. Meeting up with the younger versions of me that I banished into the wilderness, in my desire to be a 'better' person. And, yes, when I move backwards and bump into my old self, I might even find myself behaving in old unhealthy ways again, as I revisit history once more (just to be sure).

But this little dalliance with my old dysfunctional self is a mere blip. In fact, just as 'relapse' is considered a necessary part of addiction recovery, I believe this applies to us 'dancing in the dark' with our old selves, too. It's nothing more than a brief backward dance step. And each time we revisit that place, we remember why we left it.

So please show yourself some compassion when you do find yourself dancing backwards. Soon enough you will return to your senses, scoop up that old version of yourself into your arms and whisper lovingly to them, 'Enough now, my love, we're heading forwards, and I've got you ...'

And then off you will go, back to the future.

Planting seeds

I consider myself an Elder in training. A woman who has lived and loved and hated and hurt. Someone who knows what it feels like to fall and to fly. Someone who has made many mistakes, hurt a lot of people (especially myself), and found the lessons and gifts along the rocky road called Life.

A woman who holds hands with her ancestors and her grandchildren. Someone who has transformed her past and pain into Wisdom and Wonder that she is ready to share. A woman still learning and stumbling.

So here are a few seeds of hope I wish to plant today. I pray that some of them will land in your heart and, when ready, you will water them and they, like you, will grow and blossom. All in good time.

» Whenever you are brought to your knees by life, make sure you take a good look around whilst down there. There is ALWAYS a gift hidden in the dirt.

» It was never meant to be easy, but it does get better. I promise.

» Every bad relationship teaches you what you don't want. Nothing is wasted.

» Grief is Love bleeding, and we are meant to bleed.

» Tears are liquid drops of Love.

» A restlessness and yearning are signs you're heading in the right direction.

» Working on yourself is the best gift you will ever give yourself and your family.

» The biggest barriers to your freedom and peace are your habitual thinking and beliefs.

» Every time you interrupt a negative thought, word or behaviour, you are building a new life.

» You really are perfect.

» Sometimes angels have dark wings.

» Everyone has an affinity with a specific part of nature – find yours and go there often.

» You will look back on this period of your life and see how it was your becoming.

» Connection is the answer. Connection with your body, your heart and Soul, your tribe, the planet, the Divine. It's all about connection.

» Love is everywhere – we just need to learn how to taste it.

» Gratitude and (self) compassion are the medicine.

» The Soul doesn't run.

» Let Life Love you.

» Everyone needs an Elder to guide them and a community to hold them. Find yours.

Judgy judgy

Most of our thoughts are not even thoughts, they are judgements.

And all of our judgements simply show us our shadow. So think about that.

Seven deadly sins for the modern age

In no particular order:

1. Entitlement – the world (and that includes you!) owes me everything and I'm entitled to take, take, take! And f*ck you, you, you!

2. Narcissism – it's all about me, myself and I. 'Look at my perfect life ... aren't I thin, rich and fabulous?!' Do you see meeeeee!?

3. Verbosity – too many words, too much talking. Blah, blah, blah, (please love me) blah.

4. Over-intellectualising – blah, insert big words, aren't I clever? Blah. I've read so many books ... (zzz)

5. Immediate gratification – I want it and I want it NOW! And no, I won't save or queue or wait my turn. Do you have any idea who I am?!

6. Giving in to the ego – I must compete and win, be right, prove you wrong, be 'perfect' and, oh yes, be *so* much better than you.

7. The forgetting – of the heart, love, Soul, connection, humility, faith, grace, truth and service.

Just for today

What if, just for today, you were to act as if everything in your life was simply perfect? As though everything happening to you, and through you, was also happening for you? Your life was meant to be unfolding exactly as it is. Imagine it. Yes, with all of the chaos and the poor choices, the blessings, the struggles, the joys, even the heartbreaks and losses ... all of it, just perfect. Imagine ...

Act for today, as if Life has your back completely. As though there is a sacred order to all of Life that you totally and utterly believe in. It doesn't mean you have to understand it or like what's served up from Life's vast 'Menu of the Day'. It certainly doesn't mean that you will enjoy its (sometimes bitter) taste, but it does mean that you accept it all, completely. Trust in it wholeheartedly. Just for today.

Act as if there was no more waiting or seeking or yearning for 'something more or better'. As though the journey really is the destination. It was all true after all. And everything you have inside of you is all you will ever need. Act as if ...

Just for today, act as if you totally believe these words are true (because deep down, you know that you do).

The art of life surfing

Life is a bit like surfing. You can sit on the beach and watch as others surf, living life as a spectator sport. Or you can take a deep breath of courage and get in the water, cold and shivering with fear. Everyone was a beginner once, you know.

Learning to surf through life is an art form. It requires practice, faith, truth and surrender. Not a single tumble is ever wasted, though. Growth. Sometimes it feels as if you fall off the board endlessly, all clumsy limbs, choking and despair. The waves will have you and drag you under. And down, down, down you will go.

And at other times (after the 57,000th tumble), you will finally surface and climb back on the board and simply glide. Perfection. Grace and grit together. It's incredible ... and oh my goodness, the views!! It's all been worth it. Wow! Takes your breath away. It's as if you're flying through your life. The water and you as one ... which of course you are. Until the next tumble!

But do you want to know the true secret to the art of surfing? The secret that only a few champion Life surfers know? OK, lean in close and I'll whisper it to you.

You must learn to appreciate the view both above and below the water.

Forgotten crowns

Misogyny = dislike, contempt for, distrust of and ingrained prejudice against women.

Internalised misogyny = when women swallow the bitter pill of misogyny whole, without chewing (or questioning), and are unable to digest and metabolise that which does not belong to them. It slowly poisons their self-worth and capacity to accept, love and adore all that they are. Each negative thought, word and behaviour bubbles up from their chronic indigestion, robbing them of their inherent Power.

As the misogynistic toxins build and build inside their sensitive system, they begin to leak out towards other girls and women (forgotten Sisters), through the rehashing of sexist and gender stereotypes, judgements and behaviours. And then down, down, down the women all fall, dragging others with them as they descend, crowns tumbling and hearts shattering all around.

Wisdom

Rather than having something missing, could it simply be that you are missing something?

And

There was a moment when I came to see that life and living are all about the 'and', not the 'or'. It was a precious (hard-won) moment when I finally arrived at this place of integration in myself and in the world.

Like many of you, I had been taught to believe only in the 'or':

This *or* that

Good *or* bad

Real *or* fake

Me *or* you

In *or* out

Strong *or* weak

How conveniently limiting this little two-letter word is. A patriarchal gift. How small it keeps us all. Especially as women. You're either beautiful or smart. Young or old. Sweet or aggressive. A 'laydee' or a whore.

And yet we women know in the deepest part of our being that we are way too big to live that small.

Or what?!

Oh, how this little word held me back from loving and accepting all that I am, for years. How it blocked me from experiencing all of life's riches. Because life (and all of us, as part of life) is all about the 'and'.

I'm happy *and* sad.

I'm lonely *and* connected.

I'm broken *and* whole.

I'm closed *and* open.

I am terrified *and* have faith.

A miraculous warrior woman *and* a moaning old Minnie.

I'm shadow *and* light.

I'm funny *and* serious.

Vulnerable *and* strong.

I am dying *and* alive.

I am innocent *and* wise.

I am five *and* 5,000 years old.

A witch *and* a wonder.

I am all that I have ever been. I am all of my ages and all of my emotions. All of life's seasons pass through me.

I *am* the seasons. Sometimes all in one day.

I am spring, summer, autumn and winter.

(Although the moaning old Minnie part still resists the cold, if truth be told.)

Soul diving

It can be fun for a while to paddle in the shallows. The ego loves a dip. A selfie here, a pair of shoes there. 'He said, she wore.' Blah, blah, blah. But sooner or later the meaninglessness of it all will begin to tug at your heart. And you'll look up from your phone to find that you are drowning in only two centimetres of water.

Your hair will look a mess as your head goes under and your shoes will eventually float away (so pretty). And then down, down, down you'll go, finding that life is not so shallow after all.

Someone you love will leave, someone you love will die. A sickness will arrive. Addiction will have you. And down further still you will fall. Until finally you hit rock bottom.

As your eyes adjust to the murky depths, you will begin to see something sparkling down there among the rocks (and old shoes). So you swim towards this tiny shred of light and discover that it is in fact your new Life, patiently waiting there for you.

You pick it up and slowly, slowly begin to surface ...

A wake-up call

There's waking up, and then there's Waking Up.

All in good time, my friend.

You're doing great.

9

Awakening

Belonging

If you are a mermaid but try to live as if you are only human, you will always be crawling everywhere, because Mermaids don't belong on land. They belong in the sea ...

Awaken

Some lies you've been sold:

» There's something wrong with you.

» There is only one body size and shape.

» You need to be happy all of the time.

» Anger is bad and should be held in or denied at all costs.

» Romantic and family love are the only forms of love that matter.

» We are separate.

» Death is the end.

» Ageing is the beginning of the end.

» You must stay young and beautiful (externally) forever.

» The car you drive, the clothes you wear and how much you weigh are important.

» Money makes you happy.

» Success is related to a career and money.

» Prayer is only for the religious.

» Your ego is who you are and your thoughts are 'the truth'.

The Truth that you hold:

» You are absolutely perfect.

» Your body is a miracle.

» Anger is the sister of passion.

» Grief is Love.

» You are meant to be wounded, suffer and heal as part of the human condition.

» Your wounds are the portal to your connection to the Divine.

» Life is eternal; death is transition.

» Becoming an Elder, getting old and wise, is one of the most important roles you will ever take on (after parenting).

» Every woman becomes a mother of some kind. She will always give birth to new life in some form.

» Happiness is paying attention to the details.

» Forgiveness becomes irrelevant when you see through the eyes of your heart.

» Gratitude will save your life.

» Trees will talk when you learn to listen.

» Praying to the otherness of Life will lead you Home.

» Love is all that matters. Your heart is so BIG, you can Love the whole world into healing.

» Instant coffee is always a mistake.

» There are no mistakes.

Good vibrations?

There is an old saying that goes something like: 'We become the five people we spend the most time with.'

If that is true, choose wisely ...

Higher vibrations – these people elevate and energise you. They are often in the role of leader or guide. It feels so good to be in their presence. They hold a lot of light, which helps to ignite yours and brighten you from within.

Equal vibrations – this happens when people are awakening at the same time. It feels nourishing and stimulating to be around them. A beautiful energetic exchange of giving and receiving.

Lower vibrations – these people bring you down. 'Negative Nellies'. They suck the very life out of you and are exhausting to be around (they're not called 'energy vampires' for nothing).

Rebirth

Death will happen to us all. It's a non-negotiable part of the deal of life. People we love will get sick and die. Sadly, we don't get to choose who, how, when or why. Sometimes this makes us so angry that we want to set the world on fire. Grief.

But we also know, on a deeper level, that resistance is suffering. Death just smiles (he's seen it all before) and then takes them from us anyway. That's the deal.

If we are lucky enough to be here for a while, we will get to die many times over. Outdated versions of ourselves will slowly and painfully pass away, like a snake shedding its many skins. The fake version, the shallow one, the people pleaser and the warrior. All will eventually die. The achiever and the strong one, too. Even the young and beautiful one. Goners. All of these versions of ourselves will need to die so that we may truly live.

Deeper still ...

One of the hardest deaths we will face is that of the ego. And, most specifically, the death of our sense of control. When that element begins to die, the ego puts up one hell of a fight. All guns blazing. Desperately trying to control the uncontrollable. Until eventually, after a bloody battle with much resistance and suffering, we will humbly surrender to our fate.

And in this moment we are finally reborn. Not like a phoenix rising from the ashes, all powerful vibrant colours, flying free. No, not like that ... this isn't Disney. More like a newborn baby: naked, vulnerable, gasping for breath and wailing at what has been lost, as we squint open our sensitive eyes and see the bright lights and warm smiling faces there to welcome us.

Alive.

Living the dream

You have to grieve the dreams of how your life could have been, so that you can live the dream that is your life.

Patriarchy – the most effective sleeping pill for women

Hundreds of years of usage and empirical evidence prove its efficacy. It's the same pill your mother, grandmother and great-grandmother took to aid their sleep. So you can feel confident as you inherit and pass on this generational legacy. It is completely safe to give to your daughters, nieces and other young sweet little things. Start them early on these meds to see the most benefits.

Here are a few of the sleeping pills currently available. And don't forget to spread the word!

» Self-comparison

» High expectations

» Judgements of self and others

» Criticism of self and others as bad mum/daughter/sister/partner/friend

» Low self-worth

» Appearance obsession

» Deflated ego

» Weak boundaries

» No boundaries

» People pleasing

- » Caretaking

- » Failure

- » Age obsession

- » Inadequacy

Dosage: take a minimum of three of the above pills (feel free to consume more, you gorgeous girls, it's your 'choice'), morning and night. Then within 20 minutes you are guaranteed to feel very, very sleepy. You will then fall into a deep, deep sleep and focus on your 'shortcomings' obsessively for years.

(Rather than awakening to your own POWER and TRUTH and PURPOSE).

New pretty pink colour available just for you, little laydees. Now smile sweetly and swallow ...

Death becomes her

There are so many ways we must die in order to truly live. Here are a few I recognise ...

DEATH of someone and/or something so precious it will shatter your heart into a million tiny pieces.

DEATH of the inauthentic self: all the lies you have lived and swallowed begin to choke you. They get regurgitated, set alight and burned to the ground.

DEATH of the ego defences: along with those lies, dies the need to be right, to fight and resist, to win, to be better or less than, to be more.

DEATH of the victim: blame, poor me, martyrdom and the inevitable extended suffering.

DEATH of your old life: out-of-date relationships must go – old ways of habitual thinking and behaving, too. Life as you know it has gone. RIP.

DEATH of the patriarchal affliction: all of our stories of fears, shame, inadequacies, shoulds and should nots begin to become clear. We reclaim our body, power, voice and worth as a form of true activism.

DEATH of the illusion of separation: of the 'me, you and us' – a recognition of the interconnectedness of all beings.

DEATH of entitlement (and its close cousin: expectation): gratitude for the abundance that is (your) Life.

DEATH of love with a small l: no giving to receive. No us and them. Learning to be LOVE with capitals.

How else have you died, in order to truly live?

Re-gifting

When I die and those who love me grieve, I know that their tears will carry me across to the next part of my onward journey. How precious to be gifted those tears of love to float upon, as I head home. Picture me floating on my back, held safely in love's ocean of tears, face turned up towards the sun. My smile as vast as that ocean ...

And all the love that they feel for me (those people that I leave behind), I will ask for them to give away. Yes. To take that love they have inside of them, for me, and to re-gift it to someone else who really needs it. I pray that they will spread the love that they originally gave to me, far and wide. Re-gifting it to as many people as possible through acts of kindness, caring, service, compassion, tenderness and joy.

May every single person who has ever loved me do that for me when I head off home. Re-gift their love to someone who really needs it ... Now, that will be a true honouring of my life.

And then whenever you, my loved ones, stand by a tree, listen really carefully ... and you will hear me giggling and cheering with delight ... YAY!

Empty vessel

If you reach 40 years of age and you're still only focusing on maintaining the vessel, without exploring what it actually contains, no wonder you feel empty inside.

(If you are well under 40, and already exploring inside your vessel, then you're ahead of the game. Believe me.)

Pandora's awakening

And just like that, I woke up. After more than 20 years of existing with my eyes closed, many of them taking pills to ensure I stayed unconscious, I woke from a deep and restless sleep.

Finally, I was able to see, hear, feel and know what it is to truly *live*. Finally, I understood that the only thing I had ever needed to remember – the answer, all along – was Love. And the route back to remembering this required opening my broken heart.

As if it were Pandora's box, I tentatively broke off the lock and chains to my battered heart, and so many emotions came flooding out. After all, it had been 20 years or more since I first carefully locked it. Sadness, anger, fear, misery, despair ... they all tumbled out of me. I wailed the grief cries of a lifetime. I wept the tears of the living.

And then afterwards, just like the calm following a storm, I met Hope, Gratitude, Joy and Love. And invited them to stay.

Death and loss as medicine

You know what made me a nicer person? What helped me become kinder, more compassionate, caring and loving?

Death and dying.

The loss of my mum, and the heartbreaking four years of watching her slowly fade away, broke my heart wide open. And I had a simple choice to make. Either patch it up with sticking plasters of busyness, drink and work, eventually becoming sad, angry and bitter. Or feel the pain of the loss completely and become grateful, joyful and better.

I chose the latter. I grieved deeply and painfully. I let my love bleed. I honoured the loss of my mum and her very life with my grief. I didn't run or turn away from it (although I really wanted to).

And do you know what happened? I became the person I was always meant to be.

Who knew that death (and grieving loss) could be such a giver of Life? Because that's what it did. That loss gave me back my life.

Faith

Maybe your prayers won't save their life ... perhaps it isn't yours to save.

But what if your prayers will mean they suffer a little less and taste true Love as they leave this Earth? Surely that alone is worth falling to your knees for?

Hidden wings

There they are, hidden in plain sight, beneath the folds of skin on my dog Jasper's back, as he faithfully accompanies me through life.

They are clearly visible on the woman who cleans the public toilets, the subtle feathery movements underneath her shirt as she smiles and bends to scrub the bowl.

As a small child, when I lay in bed too afraid to sleep, an angel would visit me and use her wings to stroke my hair. She even told me her name. Corinne.

The 'stranger' who sat next to me on the bench when I contemplated suicide as a young, desperate sleep-deprived mother. 'It's tough,' she said, 'but it gets better, I promise.' And as her invisible wings unfurled around my slumped shoulders, I believed her.

I heard hidden wings gently flapping as the hospice nurse administered morphine to my dying mother.

When alone and really sick with Covid, I felt the presence of something 'bigger than us' sit down next to me on my bed, and I just knew that my hand was being held. I felt the warmth of Divine Love revive me.

So, yes, it's true, I do believe in angels. How about you?

Humility Street

'Get down on your knees,' said the Universe.

'I DON'T BELIEVE IN GOD!' shouted Ego.

'I wasn't talking to you,' replied the Universe ... 'Get down on your knees ...'

'But I don't remember how ...' whispered Wisdom. 'Can you help me?'

'Start there, on your knees ... and take a good, long look among the rubble of your life. Not at the actual broken pieces, but at what lies in between them, holding them all together ...'

'WHAT NONSENSE!!' bellowed Ego.

'SSSHHH!' replied Wisdom, on her knees. 'I don't see anything exactly, but I can feel it ...'

'What is it that you feel?' asked the Universe.

'The most Immense Deep Unconditional Love ...' replied Wisdom.

'Ahhh, so you've found her, then?' said the Universe.

'Who?!' asked Wisdom.

'God ...'

Free

If you catch a butterfly and put it in a jar, it will die, because beauty like that was always meant to fly ...

Self-care vs radical self-care

Self-care

A day-by-day, moment-by-moment choice to prioritise our own needs as much as we do those of others. It is about committing to carving out time (however difficult) to rest, play and nurture ourselves. Not always easy if we come from a past of neglect and abandonment, and have grown used to ignoring our own needs. Some of us don't even believe we are worthy of such tenderness. Only when we grieve our past does self-care become fully possible. We can finally stop abandoning ourselves and slowly begin the process of learning how to love ourselves. Warts and all.

Radical self-care

This is for those days (or weeks, months) when life hits us hard. A dark night of the Soul. Someone we love leaves or hurts us. Our inner child is triggered and we feel totally alone. Or perhaps we are simply exhausted from overwork and meeting other people's needs. Our tank is empty.

Eventually, we press pause on life and offer ourselves some serious tender loving care. This might involve a duvet, tears, films, walking, good food and daytime sleeping. Radical self-care may also involve cancelling work or social plans, tightening boundaries, letting go of the illusion of control. Asking for help. Prayer.

It is ultimately about showing up for ourselves, reminding ourselves that we are worth it and worthy. It is, in fact, a profound act of love.

And so the next stage begins ...

Imagine

Imagine if those kind words you dare to speak to a stranger today might save their life. Or yours. Or that the smile you offer someone on the street is enough to keep them from hurling themselves under a bus.

What if the heartfelt appreciations you offer someone today mean that they will cry a little less in the toilet? Imagine every conscious act of kindness supporting healing in the whole world ... because it does.

Imagine you switch off your gadgets tonight and simply tell those people close to you that you love them, and why. What if you whispered the words, 'I'm sorry' as often as you said, 'I'm right'? What if a life in service to others was the only pill you will ever need to swallow?

And imagine that the cup of coffee and sandwich you will buy to give to a homeless person today is a sacred offering at the feet of God ... because it is.

Imagine.

Echoes

If you sing your prayers long enough to your Ancestors, you will eventually be able to clearly hear them singing right back. All in the same voice.

Your own.

Returning to the fire ...

As you carefully stand up from the fire and stretch your arms and legs, you can feel the wisdom of all the words graciously shared reverberating inside of you, blending with your own. It's like the words you have heard, here at the fire, have been the medicine you have longed for. They have helped you to reconnect to your own deeply intuitive female wisdom. It begins to flow through your body, and you feel the nourishment you have received landing inside your heart and your very bones. Changing you, expanding, deepening and guiding you. Helping you to remember what you have never really forgotten.

You look around at your invited friends and family, your tribe, still sitting by the fire, but this time you see them through your new awakening eyes. Nothing remains the same. Everyone and everything looks brighter to you. More vibrant somehow. You feel the earth beneath you and the trees alongside you. The sky seems to be even more expansive than before you began. You turn towards the wise Elder and smile warmly as you humbly bow to give your thanks. No words are needed to pass between you. As you do this, she gently disappears, returning to her place in the natural order of things.

The time has come and, in this moment, you feel a new readiness. (Even if you're not sure yet for what.) You reach for your loved ones and invite them to stand up around the fire with you. You can hear the slow, steady drumbeat of your own Soul getting louder and stronger. Slowly but surely, your hips begin to sway.

Now is the time for dancing ...

Acknowledgements

My first taste of Eldership wisdom came to me, and through me, in nature. So I wish to begin by offering my heartfelt gratitude to the great mother herself. Mother Earth. There is not a hurt or heart-break inside of me that has never been soothed or healed by the abundance and medicine of the natural world. From the trees to the flowers, the ocean, the bees, the mountains and even the spiders. Thank you, thank you, thank you. Your deep and ancient wisdom has saved me many times and helped bring me back to myself. I am yours.

Heartfelt gratitude goes out to my Ancestors, without whom I would not be here. I am who I am because of you. Despite not having obvious Elders in my own life until recently, I recognise that I am in fact being eldered all the time, through you. I remember this most as I do my daily walking prayers and can feel that my feet are also yours. My hands, arms, and legs too. Every part of me. I know you are always with me and that in moments of pain and confusion in my life, I have always felt my hand being held, and then known what to do (or not to do). I also feel your unexpressed joy flooding through me and that the tears I cry belong to you too. I am being eldered by you, my Ancestors, and this is medicine to my Soul. I bow my head to honour you.

To my parents – Julie and Albert. What rich and abundant gifts you gave me. Even those ones wrapped with a turd for a bow. For you, for us and for my very life, I'm so grateful. 'I'm sorry, please forgive me, thank you, I love you.'

To my favourite sister Corinne, who eldered me from the very beginning. 'You are the wind beneath my bingo wings.' Thank you.

My daughters – Gemma and Lucy. I love you more than words can say.

My grandsons – Louis, Theo and Jax. Thank you for showing me the way. There are no words to express how much I love you. If you look closely, you will always find me in the trees.

To all the many women who have eldered me through their work (directly or indirectly), and shared their hard-won wisdom with me, including Quanita Roberson, Maya Angelou, Oprah Winfrey, Mary Oliver, Clarissa Pinkola Estés and Caroline Myss to name but a few.

To my 'adopted sisters' – friends that have become like family to me, including Gabi, Vinny, Freddy and Fearne. Also, Lilliana, Gill, Foxy, Michelle, Jasmin and Jill. Oh and Simon and Lucas you too, my honorary sisters!

Deepest gratitude to my agent Valeria Huerta for truly seeing me and helping guide me along the way. Thanks also to the amazing Lizzy at Ebury – from the very beginning I knew you would 'get it'. Thank you for everything.

Everyone at Ebury and Happy Place books – thanks for all your support and expertise.

Thank you to the book cover designer and incredible artist Danica Gim.

A bow of deep gratitude to the numerous clients, colleagues, angels, Elders and teachers that have guided me along the way, including my beloved dog Jasper.

And finally, to every woman who has ever felt 'broken' by life. That might be you.

Know that you are loved and you are not broken. You're whole. Always have been, always will be. Now take a deep breath and swim towards the light ...

In Love and Service
Donna Lancaster – Trainee Elder